Library of Congress Catalog Card No: 77-9198
ISBN: 87491-188-5

ACROPOLIS BOOKS LTD.
Colortone Building, 2400 17th St., N.W.
Washington, D.C. 20009

Printed in the United States of America by
COLORTONE PRESS, Creative Graphics Inc.
Washington, D.C. 20009

PRO
FOOTBALL
AT ITS
BEST

Compiled and Edited by
Jack Fleischer
Foreword by Pete Rozelle

ACROPOLIS BOOKS LTD.
Washington, D.C. 20009

The Greatest Games
By
15 Top Coaches

George Allen
Paul Brown
Weeb Ewbank
Chuck Fairbanks
Sid Gillman
Otto Graham
George Halas
Tom Landry
John Madden
Ted Marchibroda
Don McCafferty
Earle "Greasy" Neale
Don Shula
Bart Starr
Hank Stram

PRO FOOTBALL AT ITS BEST

The Greatest Games By 15 Top Coaches

Dedication

To the nation's high school football coaches—the unheralded
men who first taught the fundamentals
of the game to today's great players and coaches;

and to my beloved mother and father,
who never understood sports
but always encouraged my interest in them.

FOREWORD

Similar to the original version (MY SUNDAY BEST), the updated and revised edition, with the new title, PRO FOOTBALL AT ITS BEST, is at once an experience in history and nostalgia, in excitement and action, and in providing one more reminder that what football is all about is the playing of the game. Too often recently the trend has been to concentrate on the other facets, the off-field developments, the non-competitive side such as labor negotiations, court cases, and similar matters.

For each of these coaches to limit his career to one memorable game is a great problem, for there are exciting, memorable things happening on the playing field every week and there have been throughout the history of the NFL. I'm delighted for the extra chance PRO FOOTBALL AT ITS BEST gave me to get back to the playing field.

PETE ROZELLE
Commissioner, National Football League

Contents

INTRODUCTION

By Jack Fleischer

Some of the material in *Pro Football At Its Best* first appeared in *My Sunday Best*, published in 1971. *My Sunday Best* had been so highly regarded by the Sports Illustrated Book Club that an updated and revised edition was inevitable.

When *My Sunday Best* was first published, many of my Washington friends were surprised to learn that I was involved in the publication of a book on football and asked how I was able to make the transition from politics to sports. They were not aware that I had once made the drastic change from sports to politics after having spent 25 of the best years of my life in sports as a writer, editor, and broadcaster.

Sports was my first love. As a youngster in my hometown of Bridgeport, Conn., I played sandlot football, basketball, and baseball, but at age 12, I realized that the only reason I was allowed to play in the neighborhood games was because of my ability to furnish the equipment needed.

Disappointed because I knew that I would never make it as an athlete, I decided the next best thing was being a sports writer so I began submitting short articles about our neighborhood games to the Bridgeport Post.

I also volunteered to assist the regular high school sports reporter in covering daily practices and in keeping statistics during a game, and a year later, when he received another assignment, I applied for the job. Perhaps the soft-hearted sports editor, Eddie Shugrue, gave me the job because he just couldn't say no to an ambitious 13-year-old frustrated athlete whose entire life revolved around sports, but in any event, I became the youngest paid reporter on the newspaper's staff.

I thought that I was the luckiest kid in the world, and throughout the 25 years of my career in sports, I always felt fortunate in being able to do work that I truly loved.

What was most surprising to me during my years as a high school sports reporter was the encouragement that I received from my mother and father, neither of whom knew the first thing about sports.

I was always afraid that my parents, like all my teachers in school, would want me to follow in the footsteps of my three oldest brothers, all brilliant scientists who received doctor of philosophy degrees at Yale.

But my parents saw how much I enjoyed my work as a sports writer, and their only concern was that I get a college education.

However, sending three sons through Yale for seven years each during the depths of the depression had left my parents heavily in debt, so rather than place any further burden upon them, I went to work fulltime on the Bridgeport Post after graduating from high school.

I hoped eventually to be able to go to college, and when I finally saved enough money, I searched for a school which would fill my two prime requisites: it must have outstanding athletic teams, and it must be very inexpensive. Ohio State seemed to fill the bill so off I went to Columbus.

My main objective in college was to obtain a sports education. Any other benefits were secondary. I wanted to learn sports from the coaches' and players' angles so that I could be more knowledgeable while covering games. To achieve this goal, I became a football and basketball manager and took special coaching courses.

Watching great coaches and players during daily practices and then sitting on the bench during the games gave me a new perspective, and I credit this experience for my later success as a well-informed sports writer.

When I reluctantly left the sports writing field in 1955, it was the result of pressure from top executives of the paper to devote at least 50 percent of my time in areas other than sports. If I couldn't spend all my time in sports, I wanted no part of the newspaper business.

I started my own public relations business, specializing in sports, but eventually I was drawn into the field of politics and an entirely new world.

In 1958, after successfully handling Tom Dodd's campaign for the U.S. Senate, I was invited to join his Washington staff, and I agreed to do so for just one year. But like so many others, Potomac fever got the best of me, and I forgot to return home.

I first served as Senator Dodd's news secretary and special assistant and later as his administrative assistant. I was in no way involved in any of the problems which led to his censure six years after I had left his staff.

During the 1960 presidential campaign, I was news director at Lyndon Johnson's Washington headquarters, and the following Spring, I was named executive director of the Democratic Senatorial Campaign Committee. I had completed the full transition from sports to politics.

Later, when I opened my own public affairs and public relations office in Washington, I found this activity rewarding in many ways, but I still missed sports.

I wanted to find some way to regain my identity in the sports world, and in March 1969, I decided to visit Palm Springs during the winter meetings of the National Football League. I had no advance plan as to how this could get me back into sports, but a week in Palm Springs during March wouldn't be hard to take so I made the trip.

One afternoon, while daydreaming around the swimming pool, I wondered if a book with NFL coaches about their greatest games would be of any interest.

The first coach that I approached with my idea was Weeb Ewbank, whose New York Jets had become the first American Football League team to win the Super Bowl earlier that year.

Weeb liked the idea and agreed to work with me on a chapter but felt he could never decide on just one "greatest" game since he had two: the Super Bowl win over Baltimore, and the 1968 NFL championship game in which his Baltimore team beat the New York Giants in the first overtime game ever played.

13

I agreed that he would be justified in writing about both games as his greatest.

I contacted many top NFL coaches, including some who had retired, inviting their participation. While some coaches readily accepted my proposal, others graciously declined for a variety of reasons. Some did not have the time; others wanted to wait until they won the Super Bowl.

It is interesting to note that two coaches, Don Shula and the late Don McCafferty, selected as their greatest games not Super Bowls, which they both had won, but other contests.

Although *Pro Football At Its Best* is a most comprehensive collection of the greatest pro games ever played and includes chapters by more top coaches than in any book ever published, your personal favorite coach may not be in the book only because he preferred not to participate.

I am pleased that this revised edition now includes the great 1967 Green Bay-Dallas NFL championship game which was won on a quarterback sneak in the closing seconds.

Vince Lombardi had agreed to do this game for my original book during the off-season in 1970, but his illness and tragic death prevented him from completing his chapter.

However, that game, which is regarded among the greatest ever played in pro football, appears in *Pro Football At Its Best,* written by the star and quarterback of the Packers, Bart Starr. Starr, now coach of Green Bay, probably spent more time with Lombardi than any other player and is best qualified to recall his coach's strategy.

In compiling this book, I completely researched each game once a coach selected his greatest. Whenever possible, I would view films of the game. I would then prepare a list of questions, meet with the coach and record his answers on tape.

Once the tape was transcribed, I would edit the copy and then send it to the coach for his final approval.

My work on *My Sunday Best* and *Pro Football At Its Best* has been strictly a labor of love. It has succeeded in restoring my identity in the sports world, and nothing could please me more.

An undertaking of this magnitude would be impossible without the assistance of many individuals, and I gratefully acknowledge the help given to me by the following:

Marge Blatt, Baltimore Colts; Allan Heim, Cincinnati Bengals; Pat Horne, New England Patriots; Bob Kearny, Miami Dolphins; Chuck Lane, Green Bay Packers; Patrick McCaskey, Chicago Bears; Michael Menchel, Washington Redskins; Frank Ramos, New York Jets; Don Smith, Pro Football Hall of Fame; Rick Smith, San Diego Chargers; Doug Todd, Dallas Cowboys; Don Weiss, National Football League; Jerry Wynn, New Orleans Saints.

Photo Credits

Vern Biever, Green Bay Packers; Thomas Croke, New England Patriots; Nate Fine, Washington Redskins; Hugh McNally, Baltimore Colts; Herbert J. Warren, U.S. Coast Guards; Pro Football Hall of Fame.

Jacket photo by Nate Fine, Washington Redskins.

PROFESSIONAL FOOTBALL HALL OF FAME IN CANTON, OHIO. Some of the coaches in PRO FOOTBALL AT ITS BEST have already been enshrined there. Many others are certain to win places in the Hall of Fame in the future.

I

George Allen

When George Allen took over his first assignment as a head coach in pro football in 1966, he inherited a Los Angeles team which had not had a winning team since 1958.

The year before Allen became coach of the Rams, they were last in their Conference with a 4-10 record. In Allen's first season, Los Angeles finished with a respectable 8-6 record, and the following season, the Rams won their Division with an 11-1-2 mark, with Allen receiving Coach of the Year honors.

His Los Angeles teams won 47 games, lost only 14, and tied four in four seasons before Allen was named head coach and general manager of the Washington Redskins in 1971.

The Redskins, who had only four winning seasons in the previous 25 years, reached the playoffs in Allen's very first season, won the NFC title to go to the Super Bowl the next year, and missed the playoffs only once from 1971 through 1976. He became the most winning coach in Redskin history and passed the coveted 100 victory mark as a pro coach.

Allen has long been regarded as one of the great defensive strategists in the game. While an assistant to George Halas at Chicago, his defensive unit led the NFL in 1963 in 10 out of 19 categories and was second in 8 others. Following the Bears' 14-10 defeat of the New York Giants for the 1963 world's championship, the players awarded the game ball to Allen.

Allen was graduated from the University of Michigan in 1947 after attending Alma College and Marquette where he played end.

He coached at Morningside College and Whittier College before obtaining his first pro job in 1957 as offensive end coach with Los Angeles under Sid Gillman.

He was born April 29, 1922 in Detroit.

Washington 26, Dallas 3
1972 NFL CHAMPIONSHIP GAME

by George Allen

It seems as though I am constantly coming up with a new "greatest" game as a head coach, but that's the way I want it to be. I don't think that, as long as I remain active as a coach, I would ever be satisfied to say of any one game that this was my greatest, and there will never be one greater.

My choice at this time is the December 31, 1972 National Football Conference championship game in which the Washington Redskins soundly whipped Dallas, 26 to 3, to qualify for the Super Bowl.

It was a tremendous victory to be able to beat our staunchest rival who had been the defending world's champions and winners of our Division for the past six years.

It was the type of win every coach loves since it was truly a team victory with offense, defense, and special teams all playing a near-perfect game. We had to be that good in order to win by a 23-point margin over a great Dallas team whose powerful offense and rugged defense had made them a pre-season favorite to repeat as Super Bowl champs.

Bringing a championship back to Washington was very exciting. The Redskins had been without a championship for 31 years when they had defeated the Chicago Bears, 14-6, in 1942. The last time that they had even played in a championship game was in 1945 when they lost, 15-14, to Cleveland. During the 25-year period before I was named coach of the Redskins, they had

21

only four winning seasons, so it was most gratifying to bring the dedicated Washington fans a title in only my second year with the team.

As soon as I took over the Redskins, I began making trades. I may have set a record in acquiring players through trades in my first two years, but I was determined to bring the Washington fans a winner as quickly as possible.

In obtaining new players, I was looking for the right kind of veterans—players who knew how to win. That was important since the team had not been accustomed to winning. At the same time, I was trying to strengthen positions where the team had been weak.

I gave up many top draft choices to get the players I wanted, and people got the impression that I didn't want to draft young players. I wish that I could have drafted college players and also obtained badly needed veterans, but since I could not have it both ways, I took the experienced players. I already knew what they could do, but was never sure that the drafted player was going to make it. Just look at the number of top draft choices who never succeed in pro ball. It's a real gamble.

We try to get our young players in other ways—through free agent try-out camps or through lower draft choices. You'll find that our squad has its share of young players, and they aren't all eligible for membership in our "Over-the-Hill Gang."

Incidentally, I love that phrase, "Over-the-Hill Gang." These are my kind of players. I have always contended that age means nothing if a man takes care of his body and has the proper attitude and spirit.

I'm over 50, and I feel as good as I did when I was 21. I jog, lift weights, and eat carefully. If you take care of your body, the best years of your life are after you reach 30. If you don't, you have wasted yourself physically.

Our "Over-the-Hill Gang" proved time and again the importance of being in sound physical condition. They won many games for us in the fourth quarter against younger players. Some opponents who felt that they could wear us out were surprised to learn otherwise.

And, of course, there just isn't any substitute for experience. The mental side of football is 90 percent of the game. You must be intelligent. You must be able to absorb a large amount of information. You must learn your plays and know your assignment for each play. One mistake at the wrong time could cost you a ball game. You must learn what your opponents do well, anticipate their plays, and be ready to make the right move to stop them.

Mainly because of our "Over-the-Hill Gang," this was a closely knit Redskin team in 1972. They were not concerned with individual goals. There was a strong feeling of togetherness that was obvious to us during the entire season.

Team play brings championships, and these were players who felt that winning games was far more important than becoming All-Pro.

These were courageous players who refused to quit when the going got tough. They were willing to make the necessary sacrifices to be mentally and physically ready to play.

And they were always ready to give extra effort. A coach is usually content when his players all perform to the best of their ability, but there are times when 110 percent effort is needed to win.

In order to have a winning team, you must have a program. You have to know what you want, and you can't change your philosophy from year to year or else you are going to confuse your players and your entire organization.

I treasure experience, but experience isn't any good unless you have the right type. I want intelligent, dedicated, emotional players.

I am an emotional person. When I clap my hands and when I cheer, it's something that comes naturally, and I don't think you should ever hold back your feelings.

I want my players to be emotional, too. I want them to have

the character that helps them overcome adversity, and it's a rare season when a team doesn't face any number of major problems.

Players must be prepared for the mental torture they must face before a game. Sometimes you can't eat or sleep. You're torn up inside.

But then when it's all over, it's so rewarding. When you have been backed against the wall and have been able to fight back and win, there is no greater satisfaction, no greater personal reward. That's what football is all about, and that's what life is all about, too.

There's much hard work involved, but whether you are a football player, coach, businessman or laborer, you cannot succeed without hard work. And you must make every day count. A day wasted is one you can never make up.

The right experience, dedication, ability, intelligence, proper emotion, determination to win, and hard work are all necessary in order to be successful, but unless you love the job you are doing, it's all meaningless.

The "Over-the-Hill Gang" that I had assembled had the above traits. Without them, we would not have been playing for the NFC championship in 1972.

During the first part of the week before the game, Dallas coach Tom Landry did not reveal who he was planning to start at quarterback. Craig Morton had started every game that season, but in the playoff game against San Francisco, Roger Staubach had come off the bench, with Dallas trailing, 28-13, and had sparked them to a 30-28 victory.

I don't know if Landry was really uncertain or not because I have frequently been in a similar position. There were times when during the early part of the week, I just did not know whether it would be Billy Kilmer or Sonny Jurgensen and more recently whether it would be Kilmer or Joe Theismann.

On other occasions, I would know which quarterback would be starting and let him know early in the week, but I would not publicly announce my choice until the end of the week.

Whenever I would withhold the name of my starting

quarterback in Washington, the news media would accuse me of playing a guessing game with them. It's true that at times I did play a guessing game, but it wasn't with the news media. It was with the opposition coach.

Being defensive oriented as I am, I know that you have to spend much more time preparing your team when you are not certain if you are going to face a Craig Morton or a Roger Staubach. Their techniques are different, and you can't plan the same defense for both.

Knowing the extra time our team must devote to preparing against two quarterbacks instead of one, it was obvious that there was additional burden placed on teams facing us when they weren't sure if they would be up against Kilmer or one of our other quarterbacks.

Unfortunately, I could not use this strategy against Dallas since Jurgensen had been injured, and Kilmer was our certain starter.

In this game, Landry had the tactical edge, and although I had the gut feeling that he would go with Staubach, we prepared defensives against both quarterbacks.

Despite his outstanding play against the Forty Niners, I was hoping that Staubach would start, figuring that he had played very little all season and would probably be a bit rusty when put under pressure by us.

There was no doubt that Staubach could be effective at times as a scrambler, but that never worried us. He would be taking a major risk each time he carried the ball against us. We were planning to force him to the inside anytime he would scramble, and then put the wood to him. We wanted to make him feel it each time he carried the ball so that he would not be too anxious to run.

Calvin Hill was their big threat as a runner. He had gained over 1,000 yards that season, and we knew that he was not easily stopped by one man. When he carried the ball, we would have to gang tackle him.

With speedy receivers like Bob Hayes, Dallas was noted for its big play. We had to take away the home run.

Most important of all, we had to stop them on the first down. Their running and passing game was well-balanced, but if we could contain them on first down, we could dictate to them through the use of our nickel defense.

Offensively, we wanted to pass sparingly and control the ball. We would set up play action passes by making our running game work.

There is no better ball control quarterback than Billy Kilmer, and no one is more effective than he is on a play action pass. Whatever he lacks in throwing the perfect spiral, he makes up in other areas.

Although I now prefer a more conservative, ball control type offense, there was a time during the early years of my coaching career when I was very offensive-minded. Actually, I would spend most of my time with the offensive unit, and defense was strictly a catch-as-catch-can thing.

But after losing quite a few high scoring games, I shifted my thinking to defense and began spending more time with the defensive units and specialty teams.

I strongly believe in the theory that the best offense is a good defense. The same holds true in other sports, too. In baseball, basketball, hockey, and boxing, you win consistently and become champions if you have a superior defense.

Those who say that they would rather lose a football game, 40-38, than win one, 14-10, are very much in the minority.

I find no pleasure in losing at any time regardless of the score, and Kilmer feels the same way.

Kilmer was the first trade that I made and probably the best that I ever made for Washington. I had always admired the way Kilmer played against a vastly superior Los Angeles team when he was with New Orleans. Even though he never did beat us, his competitiveness and leadership impressed me, and if he had been available when I was with the Rams, I would have taken him then.

They tell a story about psychological tests that were given to New Orleans players before the start of one of their seasons, and the report on Kilmer was that he was so courageous that he would have been a great kamikaze pilot. It also was reported by the psychologist that he was so cool under pressure that if a group was sitting in a building during an earthquake, he would be calm and keep the others from panicking.

Now that may be an exaggeration of some sort, but there is no question in my mind as to the courage and coolness of Kilmer as a quarterback. He is a completely dedicated player; he doesn't know the meaning of the word "quit"; he is tough; he plays when he's hurt; he knows how to prepare for a game; he plays intelligent football; he plays winning football. Put that all together and you've got a great quarterback and a great person.

It's little wonder that most NFL coaches have said that the one quarterback they would rather not face in any one big game is Billy Kilmer.

I kept our practices fairly short the week before the game. We had looked sharp in beating Green Bay, 16-3, in the playoffs the week before, and I felt that we had regained the momentum that we had lost in dropping the last two games of the regular season.

But while our practice sessions might have been a bit shorter than usual, our coaching staff worked late every night, checking and re-checking films and discussing our game plans. Nothing can be left to chance in any football game, whether it's for the championship or not.

I don't remember if any of our practices were closed to reporters that week, but it's very likely that we did practice in secret at least once.

When I was at Los Angeles, I never had any closed practices, but in Washington, I was forced to bar reporters from some of our sessions because they felt it was their duty to write about everything they saw.

If we were working on an option pass play, they would write about it, and since stories like that would affect our strategy, I was given no choice but to close some of our work-outs. It just would not make good sense to work hard on something you want to use to surprise your opposition and then have them read about it in the newspapers.

Practicing on the field is actually only a small part of our preparation for a game. It usually doesn't last more than two hours a day. However, the mental preparation never stops. Teams are beaten because they are not mentally and emotionally ready to play and not because they are not in proper physical condition.

I believe that I reminded my players every day how important the Dallas game was to us. I happen to disagree with those who say that professional football players do not need motivation before a big game. Everyone needs motivation in order to succeed whether you are an athlete, a doctor, a salesman, a mechanic, or a painter. You just can't sit back and take anything for granted.

I felt that we could beat Dallas, but we would have to play aggressive, basic football. We had beaten them, 24-20, earlier in the season after trailing 20-7, and then after we had clinched the Division title, we lost to them in Dallas, 34-24.

As the players dressed before the game, it was obvious that they were very tense, and that's always a good sign. I knew that they were ready to play.

As a matter of fact, I was pretty tense myself. Edward Bennett Williams, president of the Redskins, brought Joe DiMaggio into the dressing room, and I was so uptight that I could hardly talk to him. I often think about that moment. I was always a great DiMaggio fan, and under ordinary conditions I would have loved to have spent hours talking with him.

The roar of the home crowd at RFK Stadium is always inspiring as the team is introduced, but this day, it seemed greater than ever before.

We won the toss, and Toni Fritsch's kick to us was downed in the end zone. Three running plays by Charley Harraway and Larry Brown gave us a first down on the 31, and Kilmer, on a play action pass, hit Roy Jefferson for 15 yards on a slant pattern. Kilmer threw for 13 to Charley Taylor on a similar pattern, and we had a first down on the Dallas 41.

Our game plan was working to perfection. We had started

out by running the ball on straight power plays, setting them up for play action passes which completely fooled them.

On third and six on their 37, Kilmer passed to Brown for a first down, but Larry fumbled the ball as he was hit, and Dallas recovered to stop us.

Late in the first period, we started a drive on our own 27, and moved almost exclusively on the ground to get a first down on the Dallas 16. Brown carried the ball on six plays, Harraway on two, and in between Kilmer passed once to Brown for nine yards and once to Harraway for seven. We were placed in four third down situations, and each time, we converted.

However, the Dallas defense tightened up on the next three plays, and we were forced to settle for an 18-yard field goal by Curt Knight.

That drive was an exhibition of ball control at its best. We had possession for nine minutes and 15 seconds. We ran 14 plays, and our longest gain either running or passing was an 11-yard run by Brown.

Dallas got the ball for only the third time in the first half, and just like the other two times, they had to punt to us after three plays.

We started from our 28 this time, and after Harraway failed to pick up any yardage, Kilmer passed incomplete to Taylor. Charley had run a short down-and-out pattern, but that play served to set up Dallas for the next play. On a "go" pattern, Taylor went down but didn't go out this time. He kept on going and out-raced Charlie Waters on a 51-yard pass play which gave us a first down on their 21.

It was another great call by Kilmer, who until then had only attempted short passes.

With a third and four on their 15, Taylor ran a slant pattern in front of Waters, and although Kilmer was under tremendous pressure, he waited until the last split second to release the ball, and we had our first touchdown at 9:27 of the second period. Knight's extra point gave us a 10-0 lead.

A personal foul against us, followed by a 29-yard scramble by Staubach, put us in trouble for the first time, but with a first down on our 28, Dallas failed on three successive passes. Fritsch then came in to kick a field goal from the 35, and our lead was cut to 10-3.

Dallas got the ball on its own 39 with 54 seconds to play and almost got on the board again. A 15-yard pass from Staubach to Lance Alworth and one for 22 yards to Ron Sellers moved the ball to our 16 with seven seconds left in the half.

Staubach's pass intended for Alworth was incomplete, and with only two seconds left, Fritsch attempted a field goal from our 23. It was wide to the left, and we took a 10-3 lead into the dressing room when it easily might have been 10-6 or possibly tied if Staubach had been able to hit Alworth.

Although a seven-point lead against a team like Dallas isn't anything to crow about, I was pleased with the way our team had played the first half. We had controlled the ball as planned and had been able to convert on seven out of ten third-down plays.

We had the ball on 34 offensive plays, compared to 20 for Dallas, and we had passed only 11 times while running on 23 plays. Kilmer had hit on eight of the 11 passes for 119 yards as he picked the Dallas secondary apart very effectively.

Our defense was doing its job, too. Hill and Garrison had been held to a total of 18 yards rushing, and except for the one 29-yard scramble, Staubach had been contained. He was able to complete only three of seven passes for 44 yards, thanks to the combination of a good rush and great coverage by our secondary.

We planned no changes for the second half. We would continue our ball control game, running the ball frequently and keeping them honest with play action passes whenever necessary.

I reminded the defense that Dallas had a lot of speed and was a constant threat to score on a big play. We had to make sure that they didn't get anything cheap.

We had to contain them on the first series because if they tied it up, the momentum could change, and we'd be in trouble. We had to play a little harder and stick together for the next 30 minutes, and we would be NFC champions going to the Super Bowl. Dallas is the world's champions, I told the squad, and we couldn't beat a better team.

Knight booted the ball out of the end zone to start the second half, and Dallas took over on its 20. We were determined to stop them on this first series. Jack Pardee nailed Hill for an eight-yard loss, and we were off to a good start, but Staubach hit Garrison for 13, and on third and five passed to tight end Mike Ditka, who was on his way to a first down when he was stopped by Pardee and Chris Hanburger. Pardee and Hanburger couldn't have hit him harder if they were trying to keep Ditka from crossing the goal line, and this was an important play for us because we had stopped their first series as planned.

Later in the third period, we had another crucial play which went in our favor. On third and one from our 32, there was a mix-up in our backfield, and Kilmer fumbled the ball. As the ball bounded towards our goal line, three Dallas players had a chance to recover but Jerry Smith finally made a great recovery for us, and it was one of those rare times when you didn't mind taking a 14-yard loss.

Dallas could have tied the score if they had recovered, and it would have been a new ball game, but we were able to kick it away on the fourth down.

When we got the ball on our 22 on the next series, we started another ball control drive. Mixing four Larry Brown running plays with four passes, we gained only 33 yards in getting three first downs. The longest gain from these ten plays was an eight-yard run by Brown. Three of Kilmer's passes went for only four yards each, and one was good for seven.

But once again, Kilmer was setting up Dallas for the big play. On the second play of the final quarter, on a third and ten situation on the Dallas 45, Taylor broke down field and was well-covered around the 35 where a completed pass would have been just enough for a first down.

However, Taylor didn't try to outmaneuver his defenders at that spot. He turned on the steam and out-raced young Mark

Washington. Kilmer, who had dropped back behind great protection, uncorked what seemed to me like the longest pass I had ever seen him throw. Taylor pulled it in on the goal line and stepped into the end zone for his second touchdown. Knight's kick made it 17-3.

From then on, we played a safe, conservative game, passing only once and settling for field goals by Knight. Each time that we got the ball after that last touchdown, we had excellent field position, but we were satisfied to get into field goal range and let Knight do the rest. He hit from 36, 46, and 45, giving him four out of four for the day.

I was particularly pleased for Knight since he had had considerable trouble during the regular season. He had been in a very bad slump, but somehow, I had great confidence in Curt and was certain that he would snap out of it. He couldn't have picked a better time to regain his old form, hitting on three for three the week before against Green Bay in the playoffs.

This was one of those games when it is impossible to single out any individual stars. It was strictly a team effort, and every player deserved a game ball. Our offense, defense, and specialty teams all did their jobs to perfection.

Even when Dallas tried to surprise our "Over-the-Hill Gang" with four speedy wide receivers, we were ready for them. We dogged them and put such a rush on Staubach that this tactic turned out to be a disaster. We just ate them up.

Staubach was able to complete only nine of 20 passes for 73 yards. There had been games when he would complete almost that much on one play alone.

Hill, who had rushed for more than 100 yards against us a few weeks earlier, was held to 22 yards, and Garrison could gain only 15.

Our ball control enabled us to have possession on 44 running plays, compared to 21 for Dallas. Larry Brown gained 88 of our 122 yards on the ground, and Kilmer missed on only four of 18 passes for 194 yards. Taylor was responsible for 146 yards of that total, with seven receptions and both touchdowns.

Fog was setting in as the players carried me off the field, and the excitement was unbelievable. The "Over-the-Hill Gang" had come through with a most impressive win, and we were going to the Super Bowl.

The victory over Dallas was such a great one for us that I'm afraid that playing Miami in the Super Bowl was almost anticlimactic. I don't want to take anything away from Miami. Any team that can go undefeated through an entire NFL season must be great, and the 1972 Miami team was one of the best.

But it was obvious that we did not play as well against Miami as we had against Dallas, and although I personally don't need the reminder, I now have a sign on my desk that reads: "The Team Is Never Up."

II

Paul Brown

Paul Brown created dynasties at Massillon (O.) High School, Ohio State University, Great Lakes Naval Training Station, and the Cleveland Browns, building championships on all levels as he compiled a record of 351 victories, 133 defeats, and 16 ties for an amazing percentage of .725.

Together with Art McBride, he organized the Cleveland franchise in the All-America Football Conference and promptly won four straight titles while dominating the league with 52 wins, four defeats, and three ties.

When Cleveland moved into the NFL, the competition was stronger, but in 13 seasons, Paul Brown had only one losing season. His Browns won eight Conference titles and three NFL crowns while running up a record of 115-49-6.

He came out of retirement in 1967 to start the Cincinnati Bengals which opened play in the AFL in 1968. Brown's ability to build teams with solid foundations quickly paid off, and the Bengals won Division titles in 1970 and 1973.

Brown retired from active coaching following the 1975 season and now serves as general manager of the Bengals.

He was inducted into the Pro Football Hall of Fame in Canton where many of his former players are enshrined.

Brown was an excellent runner and passer at Miami (O.). His first coaching job was in 1930 at Maryland's Severn Prep. In two seasons, his teams won 16, lost one, and tied one before he was called to Massillon where he won national fame with his great high school teams.

His 1942 Ohio State team won the national championship.

Cleveland 30, Los Angeles 28
1950 NFL CHAMPIONSHIP GAME

by Paul Brown

I feel that I am an extremely fortunate man. While so many individuals must grind out a livelihood working at a job in which they have little or no interest, I have spent my lifetime in football, thoroughly enjoying every minute of it.

I never looked at coaching as a job. It has always been something that fascinated me, whether it was at Severn Prep near Annapolis, Massillon High School, Ohio State University, the Great Lakes Naval Training Station, the Cleveland Browns, or the Cincinnati Bengals.

Other than my family, I have had no major interest except football. I have been completely dedicated and consumed by the game. I was fortunate that my entire family was just as interested in my profession. They were literally raised to be a part of it. It was their life, too. We never considered our profession as being a hardship on our family life because they were a part of it.

To become a success as a coach, you must have good players and a solid organization. When the Cleveland Browns received a franchise in the All-American Conference in 1946 and I was named to coach the team, we hand-picked every player for that team, and many of them remained for many years to become what some considered one of football's great dynasties.

Some of these players had been on our teams at Massillon High, Ohio State, or Great Lakes. Others had played against our teams. These players were selected not only because of their skills but also because of their intelligence, dedication, and unselfishness.

We were always searching for players who were interested in much more than collecting a pay check. We wanted players willing to make the necessary sacrifices to reach the top, players who had the desire to win, players who put team accomplishments ahead of individual records.

The personality of the players was important to us. We wanted high calibre individuals whom we could respect. Their activities off the field were important to us since it had a great deal to do with their performance on the field.

I admit that I was personally demanding of our players, but I don't feel that I was ever unreasonable. Some players might have been unhappy about our strict rules and regulations, but despite occasional griping, my players must have realized that these rules were established for their own good and the welfare of the team. I don't think that I was forced to levy fines for violation of these rules more than two or three times during all my years as coach of the Browns.

I made my players train hard in order to get them into top physical condition to enable their bodies to endure the rigors of a long, difficult season. In order to win championships, they had to be as strong during the final quarter of the last game of the season as they were in the first quarter of the opening game.

I was equally concerned about the mental training of my players who were required to take notes during every meeting with my coaches or myself. Later, I would test and grade them to make sure that they had absorbed what we were trying to teach them.

I was simply using standard classroom techniques to help their learning process. By writing down everything they were told, they were less apt to forget what they had been taught. It is one of the laws of learning.

In football, there is no room for mistakes. Players must execute their assignments with precision, and this can be accomplished only if the players have complete knowledge of what they are supposed to do and why they are supposed to do it.

Although I had been a quarterback and many of my teams at

Cleveland were great offensive teams, I never emphasized offense at the expense of defense. It was an overall proposition. You needed a good defen e and special teams as well as a solid offense.

And, of course I always regarded the kicking game as a very vital part of all our teams. We could be great on offense and defense, but where would we have been without a place kicker like Lou Groza or a punter like Horace Gillom?

We picked our quarterbacks not just for their ability to pass but for their intelligence and leadership as well.

Some will ask why, if I picked my quarterbacks for their intelligence, didn't I allow them to call their own plays? First, let me emphasize that I regarded Otto Graham as one of the most intelligent players that I have ever coached, but his intelligence had nothing to do with my decision to call plays.

Having played quarterback, I knew how much concentration it took just to call the plays. And most important of all, your back was to the line of scrimmage when handling the ball on a running play. You couldn't possibly see as much as coaches could from their various vantage points.

Also, when you and your coaches in the stands know what play is being called, you know what to watch for. Each of us watch certain areas, making it possible for us to see every part of the play. It's like an instant replay for the coach.

If a play fails, we can tell immediately what went wrong, and we might be able to make proper adjustments and use the play with success the next time.

If the coach on the sidelines can't see what happened on a play, the coach in the end zone might. The coaches in the end zone are especially helpful to our pass offense because they can watch the seams of the opponent's zone open. They also can detect if the receiver is able to get a yard or two lead against a man-to-man defender.

The coaches have all our game plans laid out in front of them, including the tendencies of the opposition. Unlike the quarterback, we can constantly check these and thereby choose the plays more effectively.

Nothing is left to chance. The quarterback has a lot of flexibility at the line of scrimmage. We even have what we call a "check with me" plan where the quarterback doesn't call the play until he gets to the line of scrimmage. This is done against various overshifts. Also, he has the usual audibles for blitzes and special defenses.

In other words, he makes many decisions, and he must be able to make many quick assessments, so it isn't as mechanical as some critics of this system may claim.

Sending in the plays relieves the quarterback of a tremendous amount of pressure and allows him to concentrate on the execution of the play. He does not have to worry about calling the wrong play. Calling the right play is our responsibility, and that's the way it should be.

It's best for the quarterback, and it's best for the team. I really can't understand those who are critical of this system. After all, it has proven to be quite successful through the years.

Ironically, almost all the teams call defensive signals, and you never hear it mentioned.

The actual success of a team boils down to basic fundamentals, and it is the responsibility of the coaching staff to teach every player these fundamentals.

A coach must leave nothing to chance, and that means he must be demanding of his players and his staff. Mistakes must be eliminated, and this can be accomplished only by being demanding.

But being demanding is not enough by itself to build a winning team. A strong organization is essential to any team's success, and in order for a team to be successful year after year, the players must answer to the coach.

That is the only way. If an owner becomes involved in the day-to-day operation of a team and starts socializing with the players, that organization is looking for trouble—and will find it quickly enough.

For many years, I had complete authority at Cleveland, and I was proud of our accomplishments. We had many great teams, exciting games, and championship seasons.

40

I have been equally proud of what we have been able to achieve at Cincinnati with an expansion team, and the Bengals have provided me with many memorable games.

However, through all these years and the many great games that I have coached, it is not difficult for me to select my greatest game.

It was the National Football League championship contest between Cleveland and Los Angeles, played in Cleveland on December 24, 1950. This was not only the greatest game that I ever coached, but it was the greatest game I have ever seen.

It had all the ingredients for being a great game. There was so much at stake, and it wasn't just the championship. It was a game between a team which had left Cleveland for the West Coast and the team which had replaced them in the new All-America Conference. Some of the Cleveland Rams players had refused to make the move to Los Angeles and decided to play with us, so there were more than the usual emotional aspects to this game.

Then, there was the incidental matter of proving to some of the disbelievers that this was truly a great Cleveland team. Although we had completely dominated the All-America Conference during the four previous years and then won our Division title in our first year in the National Football League, there still were some writers and fans around the country who refused to believe that we were for real.

If we could beat Los Angeles for the world pro-football championship, no one could have any doubts about us. The Rams were considered one of the greatest offensive teams ever assembled in the NFL. In scoring 466 points in 12 games during the regular 1950 season, they had beaten Baltimore, 70-27; Detroit, 65-24; Philadelphia, 56-20; and Green Bay, 51-14 and 45-14. They rolled up 5,425 yards in total offense.

They finished their season with a 9-3 record, tied with the Chicago Bears who had beaten them twice during the regular season. In the playoffs, the Rams came through, 24-14, to win their Division title.

We compiled a 10-2 record, starting with an impressive 35-10 win over the defending champion Philadelphia Eagles in our season opener, and losing our only two games to the New York Giants, 6-0 and 17-13. The Giants also finished 10 and 2 for the season, but we beat them in the playoffs, 8-3.

Both Cleveland and Los Angeles had line-ups which resembled more of an All-Star game. I am not certain, but I believe that more future Pro Football Hall of Famers participated in this game than in any other championship game. Len Ford, Otto Graham, Lou Groza, Dante Lavelli, Marion Motley, and Bill Willis of our team wound up in Canton's Hall of Fame. (Editor's note: Coach Brown also did.) For the Rams, Tom Fears, Elroy Hirsch, Norm Van Brocklin, and Bob Waterfield became Hall of Famers. Others who played in that game will eventually be selected for this great honor.

Against two top quarterbacks like Waterfield and Van Brocklin, and great receivers like Fears and Hirsch, we went into the game knowing that we had to stop the bomb. Fears had caught 18 passes in one game against Green Bay, a record which still stands. Hirsch caught 11 consecutive passes in one game.

Much of our defensive plans for that game have dimmed over the years, but I do remember that we had planned to put a big rush on their passer to try to eliminate the big play.

We went into the game with the idea of controlling the ball as much as we could—not to get rich, as we called it, but to keep possession.

Neither our defensive nor offensive plans turned out the way that we had wanted them, but we sure produced one great game with any number of great plays.

Our day-to-day schedule the week before the Los Angeles game was no different than for any other game. As a matter of fact, I have always followed the same schedule in preparation for a game, and to this day, Bill Johnson, who succeeded me as coach at Cincinnati, follows this same routine. I learned through the years that players react more favorably on the practice field when they know exactly what they are supposed to do each day at a certain time. It helps their concentration.

On Mondays, the players would just jog around on their own while the coaching staff studied films of our opponent; on

Tuesdays, we would meet with the players for the first time, show them film of our last game and analyze the film; Wednesday was our offensive day and we would concentrate on our offensive plans; Thursday, we would work with our defensive unit; Friday was our combination day, finalizing our plans with our special teams; Saturday would be a short session, mainly to loosen up.

I recall that there was tenseness among the players the week before the Los Angeles game, but this was understandable. This was the big moment—the moment of truth, so to speak. Prestige and money were on the line. Nobody wanted to make the big mistake which would louse up the whole year. Because of all this, it became a little brittle out there.

I knew the team was ready to play for keeps on Thursday when the defensive players asked me to have the offense run all out against them for a few plays. Whenever this would happen, I knew the players were ready to give it everything they had.

No need for any speeches to arouse them. The emotions were there by nature. Besides, giving an emotional speech was never my way of handling a team. It's how you act all week that counts. I never did anything or said anything just for the effect. If I didn't really feel it, if it didn't come naturally, if I didn't really mean it, I wouldn't say it.

You don't accomplish anything by shouting and harranguing and going through a lot of histrionics. We've got a sophisticated society today. You don't fool anyone. You don't mislead anyone. You can't lie to them. It just doesn't work. You have got to be open. Give them a square deal. Be honest and they'll respect you.

I was never one to rant or rave at my players. If a player did something that was wrong, I am told that I would just look at him as he came off the field and never say a word. I am sure that he got the message.

Football players, more than any other athletes, must get themselves emotionally ready to play every game. It's a mark of a pro. They knew from the start when they joined our organization what was expected of them.

Other than reviewing our game plan, I said little to the

players before they took the field against the Rams. I sent the players out to test the frozen field and allowed each player to make his own decision whether he would wear tennis shoes or cleats. Most chose tennis shoes.

I knew from a weather standpoint how important a factor the wind could be in the Cleveland Stadium and discussed this with Lou Groza before the toss of the coin. We decided that if we won the toss we would give up the option of receiving the ball in favor of having the wind at our back.

Actually, I am always nervous and on edge when the opposition has the ball. I am more at ease when we have possession, and I am calling the plays, but feelings were so tense and high that we wanted to give them the chance to make the first mistake.

The only trouble with that strategy was that we made the first mistake. On the very first play from scrimmage, Waterfield passed from his own 18 to Glenn Davis on the Rams' 45, and there was a mix-up on our coverage, allowing Davis to make an easy catch and run the rest of the way for a touchdown. This 82-yard completion set a record for an NFL championship game which still stands today.

After only 27 seconds of play, we were behind 7-0, and it was the result of the big play we knew we had to stop in order to win. However, we were soon right back in the ball game, taking the kickoff and moving 72 yards for the score. Graham completed two passes to Dub Jones and Dante Lavelli and then carried the ball himself to the Rams' 32 on a 22-yard run.

The touchdown came on a perfectly executed 32-yard pass to Jones, who had moves as good as any receiver. He delayed his start, then broke down field into the open, and the score was tied after Groza kicked the extra point.

It was a brand new game, but not for long. Los Angeles came right back, combining some excellent running with Waterfield's superb passing. Fears grabbed two passes for 49 yards and Vitamin Smith picked up 15 yards on a fine run, and those three plays helped put them down on our 4-yard line. Dick Hoerner went over from there. Waterfield kicked the extra point, and we were behind, 14-7.

On their first two possessions, the Rams had scored almost at will against our tough defense. They were every bit as awesome as their record had indicated. Despite freezing weather, snow flurries, and a strong wind against him, Waterfield was passing as though he were playing under perfect conditions.

We were unable to do too much until midway through the second period when Lavelli maneuvered himself between two Los Angeles defenders to take a 27-yard pass from Graham on the 8-yard line and then score our second touchdown.

On the try for the extra point, the snap from center was a little high and being as cold as it was, Tommy James had trouble handling the ball. He bobbled it, tried to run and then failed on a desperation pass into the end zone.

We went into the dressing room at halftime, trailing, 14-13. As always, our offensive team went into one room and our defensive unit into another to discuss with the coaches what had been working best and what had hurt them the most.

We went over the missed coverage on the first touchdown pass. The coverage was a little late, and Glenn Davis was not one to whom you could give even one step.

The Rams were using the umbrella-type defense which all teams had used against us since the Giants had beaten us earlier in the season. It was actually a 5-3-3 defense with the three linebackers in an uneven alignment. This was supposed to be effective against Graham's sideline passes, but he wasn't having much trouble against this defense so we didn't have to make any adjustments.

Offensively, we had operated most of the first half with Rex Baumgardner and Dub Jones as flankers, and we were satisfied with the results. Although it left only Marion Motley in the backfield with Graham, we wanted to use double flankers because of the treacherous footing. By setting Baumgardner and Jones out wide, it avoided some slipping and could get them out on pass patterns much quicker.

45

There was almost a relaxed atmosphere in the dressing room. Nothing emotional was said. There was no need since the players were as high as you could want them.

They acted that way, too, at the start of the second half as we scored in less than four minutes to take a 20-14 lead. Gillom, who not only was a great punter but a first rate tight end, set up the score with a 29-yard gain on a screen pass, and Lavelli caught his second toughdown pass of the game on a 39-yard play. Lavelli, with as sure a pair of hands as any man, beat Tom Keane on a post pattern and although Keane came close to tipping the ball on the 10-yard line, Lavelli hauled it in and scored. All you had to do is give Lavelli one step, and that's all he needed because Graham was that accurate.

Our lead did not last long. Waterfield completed three passes to Fears and Smith for a first down on our 17, and we were in trouble again. Hoerner carried the ball on seven consecutive plays—most unusual when you had a passer like Waterfield—and he finally went over from the one. Waterfield's kick put them ahead, 21-20.

In less than a minute the Rams scored once again, and we were trailing, 28-20. On the first play from scrimmage after the kickoff, Marion Motley took a hand-off from Graham, slipped and was chased back from the 20 to the seven where he fumbled when hit from both sides by defensive ends Jack Zilly and Larry Brink. Brink picked up the ball and went in for the touchdown.

It was the second cheap touchdown that we had given them and was unusual for us because we normally didn't make that many big mistakes.

Late in the third quarter, Warren Lahr intercepted a Waterfield pass on our own 35 and that seemed to give us a spark. Graham was at his best during this drive as he completed nine passes, five in a row to Lavelli.

These were not set plays with Lavelli as the primary receiver. It just happened that he was able to outmaneuver his coverage, and Graham was never one to miss a man who was open.

The 19-yard touchdown pass to Baumgardner was Graham's

fourth of the game, and it was one of the greatest catches you would ever want to see. Rex made an unbelievably difficult diving catch in the end zone. Groza's extra point left us one point behind, 28-27.

We had another chance after an exchange of punts when Tommy Thompson intercepted a Waterfield pass, but we lost that opportunity when Graham, after a seven-yard gain, fumbled on the Rams' 24.

Only two minutes of play remained when the Rams were forced to kick to us, and Waterfield, who had put us in a hole all day long with his punting average of 50 yards, got off another great one to our 16. This time Cliff Lewis was able to return the punt 16 to our 32, and we got set for what appeared to be our last chance.

Like every player on our team, I had the greatest confidence in Graham. Somehow, our team always felt that no matter what the situation was, Otto would always pull us through.

Graham ran for 14 yards on the first play, putting us in excellent field position on the 46. He passed to Baumgardner to the Rams' 39 and then for 16 more to Jones on the 23. There were 45 seconds to play, and Graham passed to Baumgardner to the 11 on a sideline pattern which enabled Rex to get out-of-bounds and stop the clock.

We were close enough for a field goal, but the angle was bad so Graham carried the ball to get closer to the center of the field and picked up a yard in doing so.

Only 20 seconds remained when we called time to stop the clock again and get set for Groza's field goal attempt. I wasn't the least bit worried about the outcome. Tommy James, who was the holder, had been my player in high school, and Groza had been my player in college at Ohio State. I didn't even think about the missed extra point earlier in the game. I had been through a great deal with these players. We had worked hard to get where we were. Everyone expected Lous to make the kick, and he did, giving us a 30-28 victory and the championship.

It was a perfect climax to a great game. We had to work hard for every point that we scored, but we succeeded in outscoring the NFL's most explosive offensive team.

It was an exhilarating victory for us in our very first season in the NFL. We proved to our doubters exactly how good a team we were.

The game not only was close as far as the score was concerned, but the statistics gave further proof as to how evenly matched we were. We both compiled 22 first downs. We had 114 yards rushing; they had 106. We completed 22 out of 33 passes for 298 yards; they hit on 18 of 32 for 312.

Graham's completion percentage of 68 still stands as a record for an NFL championship game.

Not only was Graham's passing outstanding, but his running accounted for 99 of the 114 yards we gained on the ground. Otto never looked as fast as he was, but he sure could run despite the fact that he was a big man.

We used our quarterback draw play very effectively against Los Angeles, allowing Graham the choice of where he wanted to run. It worked because we kept flaring everybody out, forcing the linebackers to go with them and giving Graham the opportunity to pick up important yardage.

In the dressing room after the game, I thanked the players and coaches for all they had done and reminded them that I didn't believe that we had won the ball game all by ourselves. I asked them to pause for a minute of silence during which each of us would offer thanks for helping us to do our best in a little prayer, each in our own way.

We all bowed our heads for a minute, and then bedlam broke loose.

We were the world's champions, and it was a great feeling.

This was my greatest team; it was the greatest game that I had ever seen and the greatest game that I ever coached.

III

Weeb Ewbank

Weeb Ewbank is the first coach ever to win world football championships in two leagues.

He won back-to-back titles in 1958 and 1959 as head coach of the Baltimore Colts in the National Football League, and then, in 1969, his New York Jets became the first American Football League team to win the Super Bowl.

Weeb is a graduate of Miami of Ohio where he was a quarterback, captain of the baseball team, and in spite of his small stature, a member of the basketball team.

He began his football coaching career at Miami as an assistant coach and spent 14 years there. In 1943, he became a member of Paul Brown's staff at the Great Lakes Naval Training Station, and after the war, he became backfield coach and head basketball coach at Brown University.

Weeb next moved to Washington University in St. Louis as head football coach, and his two-year record of 14-4 was the best the school had enjoyed in 30 years.

He became Paul Brown's line coach at Cleveland in 1949 and remained in that capacity with some of Cleveland's greatest teams.

In 1954, when he was named Baltimore's head coach, he took a Colt team which was one of the worst in pro football and within six seasons produced two championship clubs. He performed similar coaching miracles with the New York Jets after taking over the helm in 1963.

Some of Ewbank's former players and associates became successful head coaches in pro football. These include Don Shula, Chuck Knox, and the late Don McCafferty.

A native of Richmond, Ind., Ewbank now lives in retirement in Oxford, O.

Baltimore 23, N.Y. Giants 17

(Overtime)

1958 NFL CHAMPIONSHIP GAME

and

N. Y. Jets 16, Baltimore 7

1969 SUPER BOWL III

by Weeb Ewbank

It was just impossible for me to select one game as my most memorable as a pro coach. It had to include two games, and I feel very fortunate to have been a part of two such great events.

How can I ever forget the National Football League championship playoff game in 1958 when the underrated Baltimore Colt team I was then coaching defeated the New York Giants, 23-17, in a sudden-death overtime that is still considered by many as the greatest football game ever played?

And equally memorable to me was the Super Bowl game in 1969 when the New York Jets, a three-touchdown underdog, scored a 16-7 victory over my former Baltimore team to become the first American Football League representative to win the world's championship.

The win over the Giants was a great thrill for me because it was my first championship as a head coach. I had been involved in championship games before as an assistant coach for the

Cleveland Browns, and those had been gratifying experiences, but Cleveland had been Paul Brown's team. Now, for the first time, a team of my own had gone all the way.

This championship was important to me, too, because it was a great team effort by some dedicated players, many of whom had been cast-offs from other clubs. The most famous cast-off, of course, was John Unitas, who was unable to make the Pittsburgh Steelers' squad and was playing sandlot ball at the time we had picked him up just two years earlier.

The story about how we acquired John has been told many times, but it's worth repeating.

It all started when we received a letter about John from one of our fans in Pennsylvania. I always accuse John of having written it himself. In any event, the letter impressed me enough to check with his college coach, Frank Camp, of the University of Louisville.

Frank told me that he felt Unitas had fine possibilities and deserved another chance. One of our coaches, Herman Ball, said that when John had tried out with Pittsburgh, he was competing against two experienced quarterbacks and was very nervous.

We decided to give Unitas a try-out, along with a large group of other candidates. It took a 75-cent telephone call to contact John, and we wound up with a quarterback who became one of the best in the business.

When I had taken over as head coach of the Colts in 1954, the team had been one of the worst in the NFL. Many changes and adjustments had to be made. I took two defensive ends and made offensive guards out of them.

Then, Gino Marchetti, who was an offensive tackle, was shifted to defensive end. It didn't take long for him to master that position as he became perhaps the greatest defensive end there ever was.

We kept experimenting with our new personnel, and it took time before all the pieces began to fall into the right places.

The team took shape during my fourth year with the Colts,

and then, in 1958, we really looked like a team that might go all the way.

At the start of the season, I told the squad that this was a year "to know and be known." By that I meant that if they knew their offense and defense and didn't make errors, they would win games and become known.

And so this squad of cast-offs and never-beens found itself at Yankee Stadium on December 28, 1958, in the championship playoff game against the glamor team of professional football, an outstanding Giant team.

The Colts had plenty of incentive to win this big one, but a team can always use a little extra stimulus. Charley Conerly, the Giants' quarterback, inadvertently helped us by writing in his regular weekly newspaper column that New York had out-gutted us in winning an earlier season game, 24-21.

There is nothing a ball player resents more than to be accused of lacking guts, and a blow-up of this article on the locker room wall didn't hurt the morale of our team one bit.

Just before they took the field, I reminded our players that they were still considered a bunch of rejects in many circles, and it was up to them to prove otherwise to New York and the entire football world.

We had a chance to get out in front early in the game as a result of a long pass from Unitas to Lenny Moore, but after we gained only five yards on the next three plays, Steve Myrha missed a 27-yard field goal.

Late in that period, Conerly got the Giants' attack moving, but as soon as they were deep in our territory, our defense stiffened. From 36 yards out, Pat Summerall kicked a field goal, giving New York a 3-0 lead, with just a shade over two minutes left in the first quarter.

I felt encouraged about our offense even though we had not been able to score in the first period. It was apparent that our ball carriers could run between their tackles, and our offensive line was giving Unitas ample time to throw.

53

We also noticed that after Unitas' first long pass to Moore, the Giants decided to double-team him, leaving Raymond Berry in a more favorable position as a target.

Frank Gifford's fumble on the Giants' 20 gave us a big chance, and six straight running plays brought us our first score, in the second period. Alan Ameche went over from the two, and we led, 7-3, after Myrha's extra point.

The Giants put on another drive, but our tough defense forced Gifford to fumble again. From our own 14, Unitas started a drive which did not stop until he hit Berry for a 15-yard touchdown. Myrha booted the extra point, and we led, 14-3.

It was a good feeling taking that 11-point edge into the dressing room at halftime, but we were not going to be content with protecting that lead in the second half. Our plan was to try to break the game wide open in the third period.

Behind some great blocking, Unitas picked apart the Giant secondary with a wide variety of pass patterns, and we moved to the Giants' three-yard line where it was first and goal to go.

Unitas sent Ameche into the line three times, but those three tries moved us only two yards. Then, on fourth and one, Unitas saw the Giant defense playing in tight and decided to send Ameche out wide on a toss-out. The Giant defense smelled it and reacted well. Their great defensive play, coupled with the partially frozen ground causing poor footing at that end of the field, helped throw Ameche for a four-yard loss. Instead of breaking the game wide open, we turned the ball over to the Giants, who after that tremendous goal-line stand, now had a psychological edge.

Some might have questioned the wisdom of going for the touchdown, instead of a sure field goal which would have given us a 17-3 lead. Well, I was confident that we could get in there and really break the game wide open. Maybe I was just a young coach who was trying to cram it down their throats. Perhaps today, knowing percentages a little better, I might on fourth down go for the three points. Your "hindsight" is always 20-20.

In any event, that goal-line stand gave the Giants a lift. On third and two from his own 13-yard line, Conerly, a great passer, sent Kyle Rote, usually a short receiver, far down field and hit him around midfield. Rote raced down to the 25 where he ran into a two-man tackle and fumbled the ball. The ball bounded away from all three players, and Giant halfback Alex Webster picked it up and carried it to our one-yard line. The entire play covered a total of 86 yards, and after Mel Triplett plunged over for the touchdown, Summerall kicked the extra point, cutting our lead to 14-10.

I was concerned but not because of the long pass from Conerly to Rote. You've got to expect plays like that to click when you have an outstanding passer and some first-rate receivers.

What worried me more than anything else was the possibility that the Giants' goal-line stand, combined with this quick touchdown, would fire them up and force us to lose our momentum. And every coach knows that once a team loses momentum, regaining it becomes extremely difficult.

My concern was justified. Our smooth offense bogged down. Our near-perfect pass protection for Unitas collapsed. We could do nothing right while the Giants could do nothing wrong.

Conerly called his plays beautifully, hitting end Bob Schnelker for 17 and 46 yards on successive plays to give the Giants a first down on our 15. Then, he passed to Gifford down the sideline for the touchdown. Summerall again added the extra point, and early in the fourth period, the Giants had regained the lead, 17-14.

Our pass protection for Unitas was not much better during most of the final period, and the clock was moving too fast. With less than three minutes left in the game, the Giants had a third down with about four yards to go on their own 40. Gifford was called on to make the big first down which might enable the Giants to run out the clock. Frank swept to his right, and Gino Marchetti got a hand on him to slow him down. Gene (Big Daddy) Lipscomb crashed in to stop Gifford, and when they brought the chains in for the measurement, the Giants were inches short.

Faced with a fourth down and inches to go from their own

43, I am sure that Giants' coach, Jim Lee Howell, did not give any thought to going for the first down. It was too much of a gamble. If they failed, we could quickly be in field-goal range.

On the other hand, the Giants had one of the best punters in the league in Don Chandler, and with time running out, a kick was the only play.

Chandler got off a good one which was downed on our own 14-yard line, and we were 86 long yards away from their goal line with only 1:56 left to play.

I didn't have to give the players any pep talk before their final chance. They knew that this was their big opportunity to prove that they were pretty good rejects, and of course, this was the ideal spot to show that they had plenty of guts. Our attitude was that we were not going to blow this game. All I did was tell Unitas to use our two-minutes-to-go offense.

The Giants were expecting Unitas to pass near the sidelines in order to stop the clock after a completion, but John crossed them up. He sent decoys to the sidelines, and fired away at Berry down the middle. Raymond made three great catches, and we reached the Giants' 13 with time left for only one more play. Myrha rushed into the game to try for the tying field goal from the 20, and there were only seven seconds left when the ball passed through the uprights to send the game into a sudden-death overtime.

I had no special instructions for the team before the start of the overtime. I felt that they had regained their momentum and knew the work that had to be done.

The Giants won the toss of the coin but our defense was great, forcing them to give up the ball after three plays failed to get them a first down.

I reminded Unitas that time was no longer a factor and that he could set his own pace.

L. G. Dupre went over right tackle for a first down on the 31. Unitas missed on a long pass to Moore, and Dupre picked up only two to make it third and eight on the 33. Unitas passed to Ameche in the flat, and Alan powered his way to the 41, barely making the first down.

Dupre gained three, but Unitas lost eight trying to pass, and we were pushed back to the 36, faced with a crucial third and 15 situation.

Unitas called for a pass down the right side to Moore, but when he saw Lenny was covered, he looked to his left. Just as he was about to be nailed for another loss, John spotted Berry open down the left side and completed a 20-yard pass for a first down on the Giants' 43.

After lining up for the next play, Unitas noticed Giant linebacker Sam Huff was a few yards deeper than usual, anticipating a pass. It looked like an ideal spot for a trap play so John checked his signals with an audible.

Dick Modzelewski charged in fast as Unitas started to fade back, and he was taken out of the play by our left guard, Art Spinney. George Preas, our right tackle, moved out to cut down Huff as Unitas handed off to Ameche. Alan went 23 yards down the middle to the Giants' 20 on as perfect a call as you will ever see.

Dupre was held without any gain, but Unitas hit Berry on a slant pattern for 10 yards and a first down on the 10.

Time was called, and Unitas came over to the sidelines to ask me what I wanted to do. I guess it was just a courtesy call since I had great faith in John's ability to select the right plays. I simply advised him to keep the ball on the ground and to call safe plays so that we would not be risking a fumble at this stage. If we did not get a touchdown in three plays, it wasn't important. We would settle for an easy field goal.

Unitas went back to the huddle and called a fullback slant which was a safe enough play. Ameche gained only a yard, but that didn't concern me. Two more similar plays, and we could go for our field goal.

Then John dropped back to pass. It's a wonder that I didn't have heart failure as John faded back. What was he up to? A pass was exactly the one thing I didn't want. Three points were just as good as six for us, and not only were we risking an interception but I had visions of our pass protection breaking down, allowing one of the Giants' big linemen to crash through and knock the ball out of Unitas' hand.

However, John lofted the ball to the right flat over two defenders and into the waiting hands of Jim Mutscheller on the one-yard line. That play took only a few seconds, but to me it seemed forever.

Later John explained that the Giants were lined up tight, expecting another running play and that he felt he could catch them off-balance with a pass. He said that he would have thrown the ball out of bounds if he had seen any danger of an interception.

I'm sure that most of the fans who had seen John and me in a huddle before that play assumed that I was responsible for the call. If it had boomeranged, I know that John would have accepted full blame, so I guess I'll have to give him all the credit, too.

From the one-yard line, it was easy for Ameche. Unitas called for our 16 power play which was designed for use against tight goal-line defenses, and with Moore leading some perfect blocking, Ameche went between his right tackle and end to score standing up.

Nobody even bothered about the extra point, and at eight minutes and 15 seconds of the overtime, the Baltimore Colts had won their first NFL championship.

For 11 years, that game remained unchallenged as my most memorable one. Then, along came the Super Bowl in Miami on January 12th, 1969, and although I was tempted to name it as my No. 1 choice, it was just impossible to select one of these great games over the other.

Beating the Colts in the Super Bowl was truly a storybook thing for me. It was only natural for me to receive great personal satisfaction in knocking off a ball club whose owner had suddenly fired me after I had developed it into a championship team.

It also meant a great deal to all of us in becoming the first American Football League team to win the Super Bowl. Before this game, quite a few football fans, coaches, players, and writers felt the NFL was far superior to the AFL and really believed that it would be years before an AFL representative would have a chance in the Super Bowl.

Many self-designated experts were saying that the Jets did not belong on the same field with the Colts, who, after setting a league record by winning 15 games that season, were being rated on a par with Vince Lombardi's most powerful Green Bay teams.

Some writers, recalling the failures of Kansas City and Oakland in the first two Super Bowls, went so far as to call this the worst mismatch possible for the world's championship.

None of these stories bothered me. In fact, I liked them. Most coaches prefer the role of the underdog. When you are made the overwhelming favorite, you are always in a position where the players become complacent and will let down.

We had no such problem even though Pete Lammons, our tight end, told me to stop showing the movies of the Colts' games so often or else our team would get overconfident.

That was our attitude. It was apparent that Baltimore was a fine football team, but from watching their films, we felt certain that they were not as invincible as claimed by the newspapermen.

There was much comment about Joe Namath's pre-game statement in which he not only said that we would win the game but he would guarantee it.

I wished at that time he had not said it publicly because I wanted the Baltimore players to feel that they were the greatest. If they became too cocky, it would be easier for us to chop them down to size.

But Joe's an honest kid, and when he's asked a question, he gives an honest answer. He doesn't say anything that he doesn't mean.

Along with the rest of the squad and the coaches, Joe spent hours studying the Baltimore films, trying to pick up flaws in their awesome defense.

Part of our game plan called for the concentration of our running attack to the left. We reached this decision in part because of the Baltimore personnel but mainly because our best strength was to that side.

No new plays were designed for our passing game. We were certain that Joe could throw against Baltimore, and although we wanted the Colts to think that we had some new wrinkles in store for them, we were ready to go with the basic patterns used during the regular season.

As in all my game plans, I try to get balance between our running and passing game, but it doesn't always work out this way. Sometimes the score or the time-to-go indicates otherwise.

In any event, Namath is pretty much on his own during a game. He is as smart a quarterback as there is in the business, and once he is given the game plan, he can be depended upon to carry it out.

His signal calling could not have been better against the Colts. He kept coming back to the plays that had been working well, and he kept making the big play all afternoon.

During the week before the Super Bowl, I kept reminding the players that poise and execution would win for them. I emphasized that they must never lose their poise even if Baltimore should get a couple of quick scores. And it was equally important that they not get angry if the officials should rule against us on a key play. No matter how adverse the situation might be, victory could still be ours if we remained cool.

The squad was told time and again that flawless execution of our plays was necessary in order to score. I warned the players not to go into the game depending upon the opponents to make mistakes. It was up to us to force Baltimore to commit errors, and this could best be accomplished by proper execution of our game plan.

We had some uneasy moments the first time Baltimore got the ball. Earl Morrall screen passed to tight end John Mackey for 19 yards; Tom Matte swept for 10; Jerry Hill picked up 10; Morrall hit Jimmy Orr for 15, and very quickly, the Colts had a first down on our 19.

The writers in the press box who had been panning us all week must have felt very smug at this point. The Colts looked like a powerhouse, determined to live up to all their advance notices.

However, our defense suddenly tightened and held on the next three plays. Lou Michaels tried a 27-yard field goal, but it was off line. We had passed our first test.

Baltimore had another big chance late in the first period when George Sauer fumbled on our 12 after catching a sideline pass. Two plays gained only four yards, and on third and six, Morrall tried to hit Tom Mitchell in the end zone. Al Atkinson, our fine middlebacker, deflected the thrown ball and it bounced off Mitchell's shoulder. Randy Beverly picked it off for a touchback.

We had stopped the Colts again. Now, it was time for Joe to get us moving. He called on Matt Snell four times in a row, and Matt powered his way over our left side each time, moving the ball from our 20 to our 46. Our game plan was beginning to take shape.

Joe mixed his plays beautifully. On third and four from Baltimore's 48, he passed to Sauer for 14 and a first down on their 34. Baltimore double-teamed Don Maynard so Joe went to Sauer again, this time for 11 yards. After Emerson Boozer gained two yards, Joe passed to Snell for 12 yards and a first down on the nine. Snell rushed for five and then swept the left side from the four for the first score of the day. Jim Turner added the extra point.

There were still nine minutes left in the first half, and when Tom Matte got through the line of scrimmage and went 58 yards down the sidelines to the 16, our lead didn't look too comfortable.

However, once again our great defense came through for us, and on first down, Johnny Sample intercepted Morrall's pass.

The Colts were still battling to get on the scoreboard as time was running out. With less than a minute left in the half, they tried a bit of razzle-dazzle on what they called the flea-flicker play.

Despite our success in stopping this play all week in practice, Morrall and Matte flipped the ball back and forth as Orr raced downfield. Due to a missed coverage, he broke into the clear at the goal line just as our lineman was catching up with Morrall. Earl apparently could not spot Orr and passed, instead, to his secondary receiver, Jerry Hill, who appeared open. However, Jim Hudson wasn't fooled and picked off the third interception of the period against Morrall.

I was satisfied with the way the team had played during the first half, but I was afraid that seven points would not be enough. We had to be the aggressor and keep the pressure on Baltimore all the way.

We had been able to run and pass well during the first half, and I felt no need to change our game plan for the final 30 minutes. Baltimore's vaunted blitzes had been negated by Joe's quick wrists and the favorable reactions of our receivers. Furthermore, if the Colts continued to double-team Maynard, Joe could go to other targets as he did so successfully in the first two periods.

I was proud of our defense. If they could just match their first-half performance, Baltimore would not be able to beat us.

On the first play from scrimmage in the third period, our defense gave every indication that it would be just as rough on Baltimore as it was in the first half. Matte, who had scared us with a 58-yard run in the second quarter, was hit hard, fumbling to us on his 33.

We moved to the 25 but were forced to settle for Turner's 32-yard field goal. Then, near the end of the period, Jim booted one from the 30 to give us a 13-0 lead.

It was hardly a safe margin, and I hoped that Namath could get us on the board again. I don't think anyone can call Joe a conservative quarterback, but in the final period, he certainly wasn't taking any chances. He stuck with the running plays which had been working the first three periods and moved us down to the Colts' 2.

A touchdown at this stage would just about ice it for us, but Baltimore held, and Turner kicked his third field goal.

It was now 16-0, but with almost 11 minutes left to play, you know from past experience that you still can't relax.

In the hopes of getting the team moving, Baltimore called on John Unitas, whose sore elbow had kept him sidelined most of the season, but John's first series ended in disaster as Randy Beverly made his second interception of the game.

Sticking to his ground game, Namath used up four and one-half minutes before turning the ball over to Unitas. The Colts then drove 80 yards, but it took 14 plays, and when Hill scored from the one, three minutes and 19 seconds remained on the clock.

Nine points seemed like a safe enough margin until Lou Michaels' on-side kick was recovered by the Colts on our 44. With Unitas—even an ailing Unitas—anything could happen.

John hit Richardson, Orr, and Richardson again, and Baltimore had a first down on our 19. Then our defense went to work. Sample knocked away a pass intended for Richardson. Strong rushes forced Unitas to throw short and then too long. On a fourth down pass intended for Orr in the end zone, Larry Grantham leaped high to bat the ball down.

With two minutes left to play, Namath used Snell on six straight running plays, and only 15 seconds were left when we were forced to punt. Two plays later it was all history.

A great team effort had proven to the football world what we knew for some time: The New York Jets were No. 1.

IV

Chuck Fairbanks

Chuck Fairbanks launched his coaching career before he was graduated from Michigan State, serving as a student assistant during the Spartans' spring drills in 1955. From then on, it was a steady move to the top.

Upon graduation, he became head coach at Ishpeming (Mich.) High School for three years and then moved into the college ranks as defensive backfield coach at Arizona State from 1958-61. From 1962-65, he was an assistant coach at Houston, and in 1966, he became defensive backfield coach at Oklahoma.

The following year, he was named head coach, and under his leadership, the Sooners amassed a record of 52-15-1.

Billy Sullivan, President of the New England Patriots, selected Fairbanks to be his head coach and general manager in 1973, and although he's one of the youngest head coaches in the National Football League, Chuck has been successful in rebuilding the Patriots into one of the powers in the league.

Their 1976 record of 11-3 which placed them in the playoffs was the best in the history of the club and won for Fairbanks Coach of the Year honors. He was also cited by Football News as "Man of the Year" and was inducted into the University of Oklahoma's Hall of Fame.

Born in Detroit on June 10, 1933, he attended Charlevoix High School where he won all-state honors as an end. He played under Biggie Munn with Michigan State's 1952 national championship team and 1953 Big Ten title-holders who defeated UCLA in the Rose Bowl.

He completed his collegiate career under Duffy Daugherty and was selected to play in the Blue-Gray post-season All-Star game.

New England 30, Pittsburgh 27

1976 AFL GAME

By Chuck Fairbanks

T he New England Patriots were a young, inexperienced team when they took the field at Three Rivers Stadium in Pittsburgh on the rainy afternoon of September 26, 1976.

They were up against the heavily favored defending Super Bowl championship Steelers, one of the powers in the NFL, and playing before a hostile crowd didn't make things easier.

But some three hours later, the Patriots emerged as 30-27 victors with a new confidence which would give them the impetus to go on and record the most successful season in the club's history.

This was my greatest game as New England's coach. Our team came from behind to win a very close game, refusing to fold under some tremendous pressure. We proved that we had the ability to defeat a team of championship calibre.

Even though we had beaten Miami, 30-14, the week before, the team still lacked the confidence needed to be a consistent winner in the tough American Football Conference, but we matured against the Steelers and followed it up with a big win over Oakland the following week.

We had an excellent week of practice before the Pittsburgh game. When we met on Monday, the team was still emotionally high after beating Miami. We reviewed the films of that game and while players who had injuries were treated by our trainer and team physician, the remainder of the team went through a short work-out.

As always, the players were given Tuesday as their day off. In the meantime, the coaching staff was working on our plans for the big game against Pittsburgh.

We didn't plan any drastic changes for the team. We were going to vary some of our inside blocking schemes to try to handle the strongest defense in pro football, but we intended to stick pretty much to our basic system.

Offensively, we wanted to go with a sound running game which was probably our greatest strength. We wanted to avoid long yardage situations so that we would not be confronted with the strong pass rushing capabilities of the Steelers.

After establishing our running game, we wanted to make some big plays from our play action passes. We also wanted to utilize Russ Francis, our tight end, who had great speed and was an outstanding pass receiver. We hoped that in some isolated situations, we would be fortunate enough to get a mismatch so he could break away for a big play.

For our running game, we wanted to avoid sweeps since the Steelers had great speed and we didn't want to take the risk of big losses or no-gain plays. We would run straight ahead, hope to achieve ball control, and then try to fool them with our play action passes.

I'm a staunch advocate of the control of the running game on offense and defense. I think that if you go through history and analyze the teams that have been successful in pro football, you will find that all had the ability to run the ball very well and thereby control the game.

That's the approach we take, but it's not easy. It requires players who are physical, players with a certain amount of toughness, and players and coaches with patience.

Although our quarterback, Steve Grogan, had enjoyed a big day running against Miami, we wanted to drastically limit his running against the Steelers, primarily because of the structure of their defense. However, we had a running play or two ready for Grogan if the situation presented itself.

Steve has great physical talents that are very obvious. He is a big, strong guy, with excellent speed for a quarterback of his size. He is very maneuverable and has natural running ability. Steve is an intense competitor, very intelligent, and, of course, has a strong, accurate arm.

Because of his competitiveness, he became the team leader and had the respect of the entire squad. But I did not know before the Pittsburgh game how he would respond under the tremendous pressure of facing the team which had won the last two Super Bowls and was favored by many to make it three in a row.

I learned that rainy Sunday afternoon that I would not have to worry about Grogan's ability to perform under pressure. He turned in his best performance of the entire season in a most difficult and demanding game.

Our defensive game plan against the Steelers centered around the necessity to cut off their running game. With the one-two punch of Franco Harris and Rocky Bleier, their ground game was one of the best, and they could murder you with their play action passes.

On first and ten and normal downs, we planned to play principally for the running game. We wanted to get them into long yardage situations so that they would have to throw, and we felt that we had a better chance of holding them down by generating strong rushes against their passes and substituting for specialized secondary coverage.

We planned to do some double-teaming of Lynn Swann, but that would be only on a now-and-then basis. The Steelers were certainly not a one-receiver team and were especially dangerous in throwing to men coming out of the backfield.

On Wednesday, when the team re-assembled, we discussed our scouting reports on the Steelers with them and presented both our offensive and defensive game plans. We had solid work days on Wednesday and Thursday, and on Friday, we spent a great deal of time on specialized or unusual situations.

We held a very light workout in Foxboro on Saturday, reviewing our game plans and doing what we call a walk-through. We put our team on the field, not against the defense, but purely stressing field position and what we would try to do with the ball in various parts of the field. We just walked through plays and rehearsed mentally our plans for different situations.

We flew to Pittsburgh in the afternoon and had a meeting for about an hour with the team, once again reviewing our plans. Our special team checked films of the Steelers, observing their returns and coverages. We also met with our quarterbacks. It was just a short, specialized review session.

Sunday morning there were team meetings again with another review of our game plans. A team must be well-prepared, and a constant review is necessary.

I'm not a big pep talk type of coach. I don't want a false or phony type of emotional preparation. Because of the close comparative strength in pro football teams, the mental or emotional side of the game is more important than in college or high school ball.

If you are at the right level emotionally, you have a chance to be successful. If you are at a low ebb, you can be beaten by any team in this league. There are a lot of home run hitters out there, and if you are off in your mental preparation, the poorest team in the league can beat the best.

I try to avoid creating any emotional peaks. Instead, I try to keep the team on an even emotional keel, eliminating as much as possible any peaks or valleys. This is especially important with a young club. I didn't want to build them up to an unusually high emotional peak before the Pittsburgh game because a defeat could then affect them for the rest of the season.

In the dressing room before the game, I knew the players were tense. That's a natural feeling before a big game, but it's especially true with a young team. I simply told them that we had an excellent chance to match up against them, and if we could play a game relatively free of errors and avoid long yardage situations for our offensive team, we would have success against the Steelers.

We won the toss, and Ricky Feacher had a great 46-yard

return which gave us the ball on our own 45. We blocked very well for Ricky, and the long return gave us good field position. No better way to start a game.

However, the strong Pittsburgh defense gave up only 8 yards in three plays, and Mike Patrick punted into the end zone.

The Steelers promptly went 80 yards in 12 plays, mostly on sweeps and pitchouts to Harris and Bleier, with Bradshaw resorting to passes only twice.

The Steelers were using a new formation, primarily on their outside running plays, and our defense had trouble adjusting to it on this first drive. Later in the ball game, we had much better success, but at this early stage of the game, we found ourselves trailing, 7-0.

On this first series of plays, Pittsburgh had been every bit as awesome as we had expected them to be.

We had no better success in moving the ball after the kickoff, but we got our first break when John Fuqua fumbled Patrick's punt, and Al Chandler recovered for us on the Steelers' 26. Three plays netted us only one yard, and we settled for John Smith's 42-yard field goal.

The Steelers were in the midst of another good drive when Harris fumbled on our 49, and Mike Haynes fell on the ball for us on the Steelers' 44.

Grogan hit Francis for 18 yards and our initial first down of the game on the 25, but the Steelers held, and Smith came in to kick a 40-yard field goal to cut the lead to 7-6 just before the period ended.

Pittsburgh had completely dominated that first period with eight first downs to our one, 80 yards rushing to our 11, three out of four passes to our two out of eight. We had failed to convert on four third down plays while the Steelers were two for two. But thanks to a pair of recovered fumbles and Smith's accurate kicking, we trailed by only a point.

Early in the second period, Bobby Walden, attempting to punt for the Steelers, fumbled the ball and Dick Bishop recovered for us on our own 42, but on the very next play Don Calhoun fumbled the ball and Jack Lambert picked it up, running 35 yards to our 22.

This time it was our defense that was put to the test, and we forced the Steelers to settle for Gerela's 32-yard field goal.

The next time that Pittsburgh had the ball, Bradshaw fumbled and Steve Nelson recovered for us on their 23.

We failed to capitalize on this break when Grogan's pass intended for Francis was deflected and picked off on the five by safety Glen Edwards, who returned to the 17.

Three plays later, Bradshaw, dropping back to pass, fumbled again and Bishop made another recovery on the Steelers' seven.

It was one turnover after another, mainly caused by a combination of some hard hitting by both sides and the steady rain which made the ball difficult to handle.

Two running plays netted us only two yards, and on third down, we lost another big chance when Grogan's pass to Darryl Stingley was intercepted in the end zone by Mel Blount.

Unbelievably, the Steelers fumbled the ball back to us two plays later. Bleier, after making a first down on his own 32, lost the ball and Nelson made the recovery.

Grogan passed to Francis for 13 and to Sam Cunningham for 10, and we had a first down on their nine. But once again, the Steelers' defense overwhelmed us, and we could come away with only three points on Smith's 26-yard field goal. We trailed by just one point, 10-9.

The Steelers got the ball on their own 44 with just 38 seconds left in the half, but Bradshaw put every second to good use to get within field goal range. With just two seconds left on the clock, Gerela kicked a 41-yard field goal to give them a 13-9 lead at half time.

Nothing is more discouraging than to give up points like that with time running out, but we were only four points behind and very much in the ball game.

Our defense had performed magnificently after the Steelers' opening drive and had forced six turnovers in the first half, but our offense had trouble putting it all together. We had some great opportunities, but all we were able to get were three field goals.

The slick field had hampered our running game. We had been able to gain only 22 yards on the ground and failed to make a single first down by rushing. Our leading rusher, Cunningham picked up only ten yards on eight carries.

We decided to concentrate our running game in the second half to our left, behind guard John Hannah and tackle Leon Gray. We still wanted to make our running game work so that our passing game on play action passes would be more effective. In the first half, Grogan had been successful on only seven out of 23, with two interceptions.

The Steelers took the second half kickoff and made like true Super Bowl champions by moving 74 yards in just five plays. A 47-yard pass from Bradshaw to Swann was the big play in that drive, with Harris going over the middle from the three for the touchdown.

For a team as powerful as the Steelers to grab the momentum at the start of the third period and lead by 11 points should have been the ball game for them right then and there, but the Patriots showed great poise and courage for a young team and refused to fold.

We took the kickoff and went 62 yards in six plays to cut the lead to 20-16. We showed that we could make our running game work, alternating Cunningham and Andy Johnson and moving mainly to the left as we had planned.

Then, with fourth and less than two yards to go on their 38, we sent our strongest ground attack personnel into the game. We even had a lineman, Pete Brock, playing the weak side tight end position, giving every indication that we were going to run the ball since we had been doing so well on the ground during this series.

As we usually did on off-tackle plays, we sent the flow of the play to the right, and the fairly predictable Pittsburgh secondary reacted as we had hoped. They came up fast to stop the run, making it possible for our tight end, Francis, to come across the weak side and get open.

He was less than ten yards deep when Grogan hit him, and he was able to go all the way.

It was a high-risk type of play for us, but it was just what we needed to gain momentum. I can remember all too well that I held my gut on that call.

But it proved that once we could get our running game working, our play action passes would be successful.

We soon got the ball back again, but this time our backs were against the wall. As a result of a personal foul, we were on our own seven, and after a yard loss and an incompleted pass, we were looking at a third and 11 situation from our six.

Despite a tremendous rush, Grogan got off an 18-yard pass to Francis, and we not only were still alive, we now had some breathing room. But we soon had another crucial third-down situation, with eight yards to pick up from our 26. This time, Grogan went to Johnson, coming out of our backfield, and it was good for 16 yards and a first down on our 42.

Grogan, on the next play, faked a sweep to Johnson and looked for his primary receiver, Marlin Briscoe. Briscoe was well covered so he looked downfield and saw that Stingley, who had run out his pattern just in case he was needed, was a step ahead of his defender.

Grogan threw a long, perfect spiral to Stingley, who made the catch on the dead run and raced into the end zone to put us ahead for the first time.

Stingley's determination to put every ounce of effort into running his pattern even though he was not the primary receiver paid off for us. We had gone 93 yards in seven plays and had moved in front, 23-20.

The next time we got the ball we went 80 yards in seven plays, taking a 30-20 lead. The big play in that drive was a great play action pass from Grogan to Francis that picked up 48 yards for us. On the first play of the final period, with a first down on their six, Grogan rolled out with an option to pass or run. When he found all the receivers covered, he elected to keep the ball and took it in himself, behind a great block from our right guard, Sam Adams.

When we got the ball on our 20 on the next series, we wanted to try to keep the ball on the ground, avoid high-risk types of plays, and use up as much of the clock as we could. We ran the ball on ten consecutive plays before Grogan passed incomplete on a third and five situation from their 19. Smith then missed a 26-yard field goal attempt, the first time he had failed in four attempts.

Our defense forced Pittsburgh to punt to us, and we had the ball on our 29 with 4:23 left in the game. We still hoped to run down the clock with our ball control, but on the second play, Don Calhoun fumbled and Ernie Holmes fell on the ball for the Steelers on our 31.

With 3:44 left to play, we had plenty of reason to be concerned. Bradshaw could break any game wide open in that time, but in addition to his ability to pull a game out in the closing minutes, we were handicapped at that stage because of injuries to our defensive backs. In fact, things got so bad that we had to use Randy Vataha, a wide receiver, as a safety man on several plays.

Bradshaw wasted no time by passing to Lewis for 20 on the first down, and after two incompleted passes, he hit Grossman in the end zone.

Our lead was cut to 30-27 with 2:35 left, and once again we tried to run out the clock, but after three plays, we were forced to punt.

Pittsburgh took over on its own 20 with 1:42 left, and every second was packed with tense action. On the first play, Bradshaw fumbled and two Patriots just missed grabbing the ball. Ray Mansfield recovered on the one-yard line, making it second and 29 with 1:29 to play.

That eased the pressure on us, but not for long. Bradshaw dropped back into the end zone, eluded three Patriot defensemen and was able to complete a 37-yard pass to Swann for a first down on the 38. Bradshaw then hit Lewis for 24 and first down on our 38. The injuries to our secondary were known to Bradshaw, and he was picking us apart.

Only 50 seconds remained, but it was time enough to get in field goal range and send the game into overtime. A 15-yard penalty against the Steelers made it a bit more difficult for them, but a Bradshaw-to-Lewis pass for 32 yards gave them a first down on our 21 with 22 seconds left.

We put a tremendous rush on Bradshaw, forcing him to throw incomplete twice. In between, they were penalized back to the 31.

Gerela came in to attempt a 48-yard field goal with three seconds left in the game.

The chance of his making the kick from that distance was not too good, but we also knew that he had the ability to kick that long.

I can recall that kick only too vividly. He hit the ball well. It started out straight with enough power to go the distance, but then as it approached the goal post, the ball started to fade to the right, and it was all over.

We had come from behind against one of the most powerful teams in pro football, sticking with our game plan in the second half. We made our running game work, enabling us to rush for 120 yards as compared to only 22 yards in the first half. This running game, in turn, made it possible to score three touchdowns from play action passes.

You would have thought that we had just won the Super Bowl from the happiness our players displayed in the dressing room after the game. Some of them actually wept for joy.

I was pleased for all of them. They had matured that afternoon into a team of championship calibre.

V

Sid Gillman

Sid Gillman started his coaching career at his alma mater, Ohio State, in 1934, and for more than 40 years has been active as a coach and executive in college and pro football.

An All-Big Ten end at Ohio State, Gillman later became an assistant at Denison and Miami of Ohio and a line coach under Earl Blaik at West Point.

His first head coaching job was at Miami from 1944-47. He served in a similar post at the University of Cincinnati where his team won 50, lost only 13, and tied one.

In 1955, he became head coach of the Los Angeles Rams and led them to the Western Division title.

When the Los Angeles Chargers were organized in 1960, he was named head coach and general manager. He remained in that dual capacity from 1961-69 when the Chargers moved to San Diego.

He resigned near the end of the 1971 season and moved to the Dallas Cowboys in a front office position.

He became head coach, executive vice-president and general manager of the Houston Oilers in 1973, and in his second year won Coach of the Year honors by finishing with a 7-7 record.

Gillman resigned following that season and is currently the offensive coordinator for the Chicago Bears.

As a head coach in pro ball, Gillman's teams won 123 games.

In 1976, he was honored by the Pro Football Hall of Fame as one of 12 coaches who have had the greatest influence in pro football and in particular in its strategy.

Among Gillman's former college players who later became head coaches were: Ara Parseghian, Paul Dietzel, Norm Van Brocklin, and Tom Fears.

He was born in Minneapolis on October 26, 1911.

San Diego 51, Boston 10
1964 AFL CHAMPIONSHIP GAME

by Sid Gillman

Many of the games that I have coached in pro football have been close, exciting ones, but the one that is my most memorable wound up one-sided.

It was San Diego's 51-10 victory over Boston on January 5, 1964, that I'll never forget because we not only won the American Football League championship but our execution that particular day was the epitome of what you expect and hope for from a ball club.

We had missed our goal of gaining the title twice in the previous three years, and each time we had felt that our team had been good enough to go all the way.

Three years before, when our franchise was still in Los Angeles, we had lost to Houston, 24-16, in the AFL championship playoffs, and two years earlier, our first year in San Diego, we were beaten once again by the Oilers, this time by a 10-3 margin.

Now, we were given our third chance in four seasons, and we came through with one of our finest efforts. In fact, that championship team was good enough to have beaten anybody in the old NFL at that time, and had the Super Bowl been started in 1965 instead of 1967, I feel the Chargers would have defeated the Chicago Bears, the NFL champions that season.

We had excellent personnel. Tobin Rote was our quarterback, and I was happy to have him with us for a few years before he decided to retire. Everyone appreciated Tobin as one of the better quarterbacks in those days. He was an outstanding talent, and I certainly enjoyed those seasons that he was with us.

Our fullback, Keith Lincoln, was as good an all-around player as any coach could want, and his running-mate in the backfield, Paul Lowe, gave us a one-two punch second to none in the league.

Complementing our running attack was a fellow named Lance Alworth, one of the all-time great pass receivers in pro football. Lance owned a pair of strong hands and rarely came out second best in fighting for the ball. He had speed and all the moves, but his greatest asset as a receiver was his ability to jump higher than any player I have ever seen. And there was no wasted motion in those leaps. Lance had the most amazing concentration and eye-hand coordination I have ever observed in a receiver.

It's little wonder that with such outstanding personnel, the Chargers were called the team with the most "irresistible" offense. We led the league in total offense, averaging 368 yards a game, and scored a total of 399 points in 14 regular season games.

Despite our well-balanced offense, I was worried before the championship game since Boston had given us a great deal of trouble in our two league games that season. We won the first, 17-13, and squeezed by the second, 7-6, in the lowest scoring game in AFL history.

There were some, of course, who thought that I was unduly concerned about the Patriots since we had won the Western Division title with an 11-3 record while Boston was hard pressed in tying Buffalo at 7-6-1 in the Eastern Division before capturing the playoff, 26-8.

However, I knew that I was justified in being worried about the Boston defense, which was the best in the league. The Patriots had allowed an average of 265 yards per game, giving up an average of only 79 yards a game on the ground. But more important than those figures was the fact that our explosive offense which was able to average 28 points a game could score no more than 24 points in our two games against Boston.

Lowe had been stopped cold in both these meetings. Paul, the league's second best rusher with more than 1,000 yards to his credit, could gain only six yards in the first game and nary an inch in the second one.

That's more than enough reason to forget our superior win-lose record and concentrate on coming up with something new against the tough Boston defense.

Boston's blitzing was the key to their successful defense. They employed a pressure defense, utilizing an assortment of alignments, and harassed the offense with a variety of blitzes 70 percent of the time. I don't think that I ever saw a team that could blitz as much as they did and get away with it. They used a combination of different linebackers on their blitzes and were one of the first teams to use safety blitzes effectively.

In planning and designing an attack for this game, we had to decide between two courses of action to follow. The first was to employ a conventional, sound, safe approach to prevent any big losses and attempt to maintain possession and position by grinding out short gains. The alternative plan was to counter their hassling defense with a feast-or-famine offense. By that, I mean gambling to take an occasional big loss against long gains or touchdowns. We decided upon the latter plan.

In order to counteract their blitzes, we were determined to use a great deal of motion against them. We hoped that by putting Lincoln or Lowe in motion frequently, it would disturb Boston's system of coverage by forcing a linebacker out of position and keeping them from blitzing us the way they had in previous games. We also thought that a man in motion would make Boston more vulnerable on trap plays, and we spent considerable time working on our motion plays the week before the big game.

I did not have to say anything special to the squad in order to get them "up" for Boston. Most of the players had been in our two other championship games and were just as disappointed as I had been in our failure to win either one. Now, we had another chance, and the players did not have to be reminded about the importance of being able to go all the way this time.

We planned to use motion right from the start on our first series of offensive plays. Boston kicked off to us, and Alworth ran the ball back to our 28. Rote hit Lincoln for a 12-yard gain on a screen, and on a trap up the middle, Keith raced 56 yards to Boston's four-yard line.

On that play, we sent Lowe in motion, and Nick Buoniconti, their middle linebacker, moved out to cover him. Keith blew right up the middle, and there wasn't anyone close until Dick Felt finally tackled him.

Lowe picked up two yards to the two, and Rote took it over from there. George Blair kicked the extra point, and we were in front, 7-0, after only 1:29 had been played.

The very next time we gained possession of the ball we were on the scoreboard again. With Lowe in motion to the left, Lincoln grabbed a fast toss from Rote in the same direction, side-stepped a blitzing linebacker and raced around left end for 67 yards. In two plays, Lincoln had rushed for 123 yards, and at 2:43 of the first period, we were leading, 14-0. Our game plan was working to perfection.

Boston got right back into the ball game, moving 67 yards in just seven plays. The big gainer was a 45-yard pass from Babe Parilli to Gino Cappolletti, who somehow managed to get behind Dick Westmoreland, and wasn't stopped until he reached our 10-yard line. Larry Garron gained three and then took it over from the seven, making it a 14-7 game.

Instead of collapsing after our two quick touchdowns, Boston showed it had the ability to come back. It looked like we had our work cut out for us.

Just before the first period ended, we got that touchdown back when Lowe went 58 yards down the sidelines after taking a quick toss from Rote. Ron Mix, our 260-pound tackle, led the play, breaking Lowe loose with a key block, and then Paul outlegged the Boston secondary. I don't think that there was anybody better than Mix in leading a toss play. Despite his size, he had tremendous speed and could run the 40-yard dash in about 4.8 seconds.

We exchanged field goals in the second period. Blair booted one for us from the 11-yard line after we had moved 70 yards to the Boston four, and Capolletti kicked one from the 15 after the Patriots had marched 68 yards.

There were two minutes and 41 seconds left to play in the half when Boston scored its field goal, and I was anxious to get another score before the half ended.

We took the kickoff and in seven plays drove 71 yards, with Rote passing 14 yards to Don Norton for the score. Blair kicked the extra point, and we went into the dressing room with a 31-10 margin.

There's nothing better than to be able to take a 21-point lead into a half-time session because all you're going to do is have some fun in the locker room. Of course, we cautioned our people against getting overconfident. You never can afford to get careless in a pro football game. Every team in pro ball has the capability of exploding at any time, and there have been teams with bigger leads than 21 points that have blown a game.

The best way to lose a game is to get cocky and then relax. The other team will catch you napping, and when you awaken and try to fight back, it's too late. Once you have lost your momentum, you're not going to regain it very easily.

I had no intention of sending my team out with instructions to play it safe and protect the three-touchdown lead. We started the second half as if the score were tied, and we planned to throw everything we owned at Boston.

Our man in motion could not have been more effective against Boston's blitzing so we were going to continue using as much motion as possible along with our fast traps and fast tosses.

However, the Patriots seemed to adjust better to the motion in the third period, and we were able to score only once. That touchdown, though, was really a beauty. Midway in the quarter, Bob Suci barely managed to deflect a pass intended for Alworth, and Rote came right back with the same play. This time, Lance leaped high in the air, made a spectacular catch in battling Suci for the ball on the Boston ten, and broke away for the touchdown.

The play covered 48 yards and gave us a 38-10 lead to take into the final period.

The game was iced in the fourth quarter when I sent John Hadl into the game, and he managed to get us two more touchdowns. On fourth and two from the Boston 25, he passed to Lincoln, and went over from the one himself, after passing 24 and 33 yards to our tight end, Jacque MacKinnon.

Lincoln had a fantastic afternoon, carrying the ball 13 times for 206 yards, an average of 15.8. He caught seven passes for 123 yards, threw one for 20 yards and scored two touchdowns. In all, Keith's total yardage for the game was 349—a new American Football League playoff record.

Lincoln's performance overshadowed Lowe's 94 yards rushing against the team that had managed to hold him to just six yards in two games. But more important than the yards he gained was Lowe's skill in luring linebackers out of position when he was the decoy on many plays.

Between them, Lincoln and Lowe accounted for 300 of the 318 yards we rolled up on the ground.

Rote completed ten of 15 passes, and Hadl was successful on six of ten attempts as we gained 292 yards through the air. In all, we compiled a total of 610 yards against Boston's mighty defense.

Our own defense, led by Ernie Ladd and Earl Fazon, who could have played on any pro team in the country, held the Patriots to 75 yards on the ground and 186 yards in passing.

It was a masterful team effort, and I was proud to have been coach of a squad that will go down in history as one of the best ever to perform in pro football.

VI

Otto Graham

Although Otto Graham is a member of both the college and pro football Halls of Fame, it was his prowess as a basketball player at Waukegan (Ill.) High School that enabled him to receive a scholarship at Northwestern University.

At Evanston, under Coach Lynn Waldorf, Graham developed into one of the great college backs of that era and climaxed his collegiate career in 1944 when he became the only athlete to be named to All-America teams in both football and basketball.

When Paul Brown was handed the task of organizing the Cleveland Browns, the first player he signed was Graham.

The rest is all history. Otto led the Browns to four consecutive titles in the All-America Conference and to championships and playoffs in the next six years in the NFL. He is regarded as one of the greatest quarterbacks of all time.

In 1958, three years after retiring as a player, Graham was invited to coach the College All Stars in the annual Chicago Tribune charity game, and the All Stars defeated the Detroit Lions.

He received a commission as Commander in the Coast Guard in 1959 and was assigned as head football coach and director of athletics at the Coast Guard Academy.

The year 1963 was a standout for Graham as a coach. Not

only did his College All Star team upset one of Vince Lombardi's Green Bay teams but the Coast Guard registered its first perfect season.

He was elected to pro football's Hall of Fame in 1965.

Graham returned to pro ball as head coach and general manager of the Washington Redskins in 1966, and their 7-7 record that year was Washington's best in ten years. The Redskins were 5-6-3 and 5-9-0 the next two seasons, and in 1970, Graham returned to the Coast Guard Academy where he now serves as athletic director with the rank of Captain.

College All Stars 20
Green Bay 17
1963 CHICAGO TRIBUNE CHARITIES GAME

By Otto Graham

There was always great satisfaction any time you could beat a Vince Lombardi team, but being able to defeat one of his great Green Bay teams that had won two consecutive world's championships has to be my most memorable game as a head coach.

It happened on August 2, 1963, at Soldiers' Field in Chicago, and the College All Star team I was then coaching accomplished this feat, 20-17, in the Annual Chicago Tribune charity game.

This was my sixth year as coach of the All Stars. In 1958, in my very first year as the All Star coach, we defeated the Detroit Lions, but if I had any ideas that beating the defending champions would become a regular habit for the All Stars, there was a rude awakening as we lost the next four years.

Actually, when I first started to coach the All Stars, I thought, as did everyone else, that we would be completely outmatched by the best team in professional football. However, I changed my opinion drastically because I learned that the All Stars, in general terms, were just as big as the pros, just as fast and just as strong.

The one major difference was the experience advantage held by the pros. Most of their squad had played together as a unit for two, three, four years and even more, and the All Stars had only three weeks to prepare for the game.

The All Stars include the best college players in the nation.

It's a squad hand-picked by the coach, and this method is better than the old way of choosing the players by popular vote.

In the years when the coach was not allowed to select his own players, the All Stars might wind up with 10 offensive linemen but none of them fast enough to be a running guard, or the team might be without a blocking back.

With the coach making his own selections, the All Stars became a well-balanced squad, capable of holding its own against the pros. In fact, I always felt that I could take any of the College All Star teams that I coached and in two or three years would have them fighting for the NFL championship.

I started to make plans for the 1963 All Star game in January of that year at the time of the annual pro draft of college players. I talked to college coaches, and I conferred a great deal with the professional scouts because, after all, knowing talent is their business. It was impossible for me to travel all over the country looking over the players myself so I relied most heavily on the judgment of the scouts.

In May, I met with my coaching staff for a couple of days. I discussed my thoughts about the squad and the game, and I set up the routine we would follow when we opened camp.

A few days before practice started in July, I met once again with my coaching staff and reviewed my plans with them.

It was not difficult preparing a game plan to use against a Lombardi-coached team because the Packers never surprised you with anything new. They did not have a varied offense or a lot of fancy plays, and you knew what to expect from their defense. Lombardi always said that you win football games because you execute the fundamentals better than your opposition. You block better than the other team, and you tackle better than they do. The Packers had good personnel, and they were well schooled. They had beaten us 42-20 the year before, and we knew that they would come back with exactly the same offense and defense. We expected the same running plays, the same sweeps, the same pass patterns. You knew what they were going to do, and they dared you to stop them. And they dared you to run or pass against them.

When my players arrived in camp, we held a squad meeting, and I outlined our plans for the game. I told them that it was always my policy to get every player into the game, but they had to earn this right during the three weeks of practice.

I emphasized that the camp would be run like a professional football training camp. We would have rules and regulations by which they had to abide.

If they broke the rules, they, of course, could not be fined, but they would be forced to undergo what I called the "whistle" drill—a physically exhausting work-out.

Getting a squad of All Stars ready for a game in only three weeks was made somewhat easier because we had the cream of the crop on our roster.

They quickly learned our number system for designating plays. It may have differed from the system some used in college, and for a few days there was a bit of confusion from time to time, with players moving to the right when they should have gone to the left or vice versa. But because they were great athletes, they caught on very quickly.

We practiced twice a day for the first two weeks and then cut down to one daily session the final week. We worked on our running plays in the morning, and our pass plays in the afternoon.

Each session would last about 90 minutes but the coaches would stay around anywhere from 30 minutes to an hour to work with individuals on their specialties.

As I look back, I can tell you that almost without exception the players who made good in pro ball were the ones who would stay out after the regular practice and work on their specialties. The players who rushed into the dressing room the minute the practice was over were usually the ones who never made it as pros. In other words, they were not willing to pay the price, and believe me, if you don't give that extra effort and make the sacrifices, if you don't work hard at it, you won't make it because the competition is too great.

During the three weeks that we were in camp, we spent many hours showing the squad the film of the previous year's All Star game against the Packers. I think that we had allowed the Packers to score five touchdowns on passes, and most of them were cheap touchdowns. We showed them where last year's secondary had made their mistakes and kept telling them to make sure the Packers earned every point they scored this time.

As part of our practice plan, we scrimmaged against the Bears. I felt this was important since it pitted the college players against pros for the first time and they could learn that the pros were human like anyone else . . . that they block and tackle the same as anyone. If they did not have this work-out against a pro team, I was afraid that they would be somewhat awed when they took the field for the first time against the defending world's champions.

Our success in any All Star game depends upon how well our offensive line has learned the fundamentals on blocking properly for the passer, giving him the necessary protection.

Many of these linemen had not had intensive instruction on pass blocking, especially for the straight, drop-back type of passer that pro coaches prefer. For example, we knew that a lineman from a Woody Hayes team could be depended upon to block very well on running plays but would not be as effective in blocking on pass plays.

With this in mind, pass blocking was an important part of our pre-game work-outs. We spent many hours in drilling our linemen in what we call "chicken fighting." You drop back a yard and hit your man. You back up another yard and hit him again. You're slowing down the rusher. You're buying time. You're giving the quarterback three or four seconds. Maybe you can even give him five seconds. That's ample time for a passer who stays in the pocket to find his receiver.

We usually have three quarterbacks on our squad. Two, of course, would be just right if they were both healthy at game time, but if one was injured during practice and the other one hurt during the game, you might as well go home. For this game, I had picked as my quarterbacks Terry Baker, of Oregon State, the Heisman trophy winner; Glenn Griffing, of Ole Miss; and Sonny

Gibbs, of Texas Christian. Those were the three top quarterbacks in college ball during the 1962 season. However, the *Chicago Tribune* asked me if I could also add Ron VanderKelen, of the University of Wisconsin, to the squad as a fourth quarterback since it could mean the sale of an additional 10,000 tickets to nearby Wisconsin fans.

Ron had not enjoyed as outstanding an overall season as the other three, but had had a great game in the Rose Bowl and also did exceptionally well in the Hula Bowl. So even though I felt four quarterbacks were too many, I invited him to join the squad, and, of course, as it turned out, he was the one who won the ball game for us.

Getting a squad of football players from all sections of the country into the proper frame of mind in a short period of time isn't an easy job, but an incident that happened a week before the game seemed to give the squad a big lift.

When we issued the play books to the team, we stressed the fact that the players must be very careful because you could never tell who might get their hands on the books. In college football and pro football, nobody trusts anybody. Everybody seems to think that everyone else is the biggest thief in the world. You have to assume that the other fellow is dishonest. It's a pretty ridiculous situation, but that's the way it is.

Well, our offensive backfield coach, Tommy O'Connell, left his play book in the locker room for a minute and it mysteriously disappeared.

Some days later, I received the book in an envelope postmarked Green Bay with a note reading: "Thanks for your cooperation. We appreciate it very much." And it was signed, Vince Lombardi.

By then, I had learned that one of our players had picked up the book, given it to Ron VanderKelen, who had his mother mail it to me from her home in Green Bay.

O'Connell still wasn't aware of what had happened, and I thought that I might make good use of this incident to build up the morale of the squad.

On the Monday night before the game, I called the squad together before our only night practice and told them I had a problem. I explained that one of my coaches had committed the unpardonable blunder of losing his play book, and I didn't know what the proper punishment might be.

Without hesitation, the squad yelled: "Whistle Drill."

Well, for a couple of seconds, I didn't know what to do. At first I thought that at his age, O'Connell might have a rough time going through the physical ordeal of the whistle drill, but then when I realized that it might relieve the tension before the big game, I told them whistle drill it would be.

Everyone stormed out of the room. The players formed a circle around O'Connell, and in cadence, they had Tommy doing push-ups, sit-ups, hit-the-deck and similar exercises at a rapid pace. I thought that Tommy was going to collapse from exhaustion, but he went through it all until I called a halt after about four minutes.

Tommy came over to me, huffing and puffing, and said: "Now, let me show those so and sos. I want to give them calisthenics tonight." So after going through the whistle drill, Tommy led them in calisthenics, selecting the most gruelling exercises—the ones he knew the players disliked the most. And to the amazement of the squad and myself, he did every one of them himself.

That night you could notice the difference in the spirit among the players. You could see that the squad had been brought together as a cohesive unit, and I'm sure that this diversion from the regular routine of the camp played a part in our victory later that week.

I have never believed in the Knute Rockne type of pep talk before a game. I prefer the Paul Brown approach. In my opinion, Paul Brown is one of the truly great coaches the game has ever known. He has done more for pro football than any coach I know. He is intelligent and highly organized. He has always been the complete boss of the entire operation, and that's the only way to be successful as a coach. Brown was never the type of coach

92

who would rant and rave at his players. If you did something to displease him, he would just look at you, and those penetrating eyes of his got across the message far more effectively than any words.

In the locker room before the kickoff, I reviewed our game plan with the team. We thought that we would have the best chance for an effective running game by going to our weak side, with our tight end lining up on one side or the other.

This proved to be right, for we wound up with 140 yards gained on the ground. That would have been quite an accomplishment even for an experienced pro team against one of the toughest defenses in the game.

I also went over the pass plays which we thought would work well against the Packers. These were mainly short passes against members of their secondary whom we felt would be most vulnerable.

And, as I had done for three weeks, I urged the defense not to make the mistakes that we had committed the year before, when we had given them the long pass and allowed them to score one cheap touchdown after another.

I told the team to go out and play good football, execute the plays properly, get a few breaks and win the ball game. I told them to cut down on their errors and just play the type of game they were capable of playing.

VanderKelen was my starting quarterback because he had won the flip of a coin. Both he and Griffing had looked the best during the three weeks that we were in camp, and I have always followed the practice of flipping a coin whenever two or more players show up equally well at a given position.

Ron and I reviewed the first series of plays that were planned to more or less feel out the Packers. We didn't expect them to use any new defenses against us, but we wanted to make certain. All during practice and again just before the game I told Ron and my other quarterbacks to size up the defense carefully and determine how they could key on certain personnel. "Find out which players can be trapped and run against them. If they are stronger to the left flank, run your sweeps to the right. On short passes, pick on linebackers who are not as quick as others. If a defensive back is laying back, don't throw long to that spot."

If your quarterback follows through with what you have told him . . . and the defense does what you expect it to do . . . and the quarterback throws the ball accurately, you're going to do very well and are going to be hailed as a great coach.

We kicked off to the Packers, and our defense looked strong, forcing Green Bay to punt. Boyd Dowler's kick was downed on our eight-yard line, and there are much better places from which to start your first offensive series.

On third down, halfback Larry Ferguson fumbled, and Willie Davis recovered for the Packers on our 11. Three plays later, Jim Taylor plunged over from the two, and Jerry Kramer's place kick made it 7-0.

My immediate thought was that this might be a repeat of the licking we received the previous year from the Packers, but you learn from experience that you must never get discouraged just because you fall behind early in the game.

It's always difficult playing catch-up football, but it's not impossible. I told the players to forget it and stick in there and get the touchdown right back.

We didn't get the touchdown back, but we did manage to get on the scoreboard with a 20-yard field goal by Bob Jencks, of Miami of Ohio. VanderKelen moved the team well on this drive with passes to Jencks and Paul Flattery, of Northwestern, while Ferguson helped out on the ground.

Our front line continued to stop Taylor and Paul Hornung, and Bart Starr had to go to the air. He found Tom Moore open down the sideline, but Tommy Janik, a six-foot-four defensive back from Texas A & I, stepped in front of Moore and grabbed the ball. He ran it back 29 yards to the Packer 27, and we were threatening once again.

After a running play failed, VanderKelen passed to Pat Richter, of Wisconsin, who managed to outbattle three Packers for the ball on the six-yard line for a 21-yard gain. On the next play, Ferguson, behind some terrific blocking by tackle Bob Vogel, of Ohio State, and guard Ed Budde, of Michigan State, scored on a power play. Being able to get a touchdown by overpowering the mighty Packer line gave us a great deal of confidence. Jencks kicked the extra point, and we held a 10-7 lead with just four seconds elapsed in the second quarter.

Green Bay came back to tie the score on Kramer's 21-yard field goal, and then we missed a chance to take the lead again when Herb Adderly blocked Jencks' 19-yard field goal attempt just before the half ended.

I was pleased with our first half showing, and I told the players that if they continued to keep their mistakes to a minimum, we were going to win the game.

Our game plan was holding up because the Packers were the Packers, and they were doing exactly what we had expected them to do. Only in this game, we were executing our plays better than they were.

Although VanderKelen had called an excellent game in the first half, this being an All Star game I had to give Griffing a chance. Originally, I had intended using Griffing in the second quarter, but with Ron moving the team so well, I just couldn't take him out.

Griffing got off to a fine start in the third quarter, moving the team to two consecutive first downs, but then Adderly picked off a pass on his own 43 and ran it back 37 yards to our 20.

The Packers could gain only four yards on two plays, and on third and six, they called on Taylor to get them the first down. However, Bobby Bell, of Minnesota, Don Brum, of Purdue, and Lee Roy Jordan, of Alabama, refused to be taken out of the play and teamed up to stop Jim for no gain. Then, on fourth down, Kramer missed a 27-yard field goal attempt.

Green Bay kept threatening, and once again we were in trouble when the Packers had a first down on our 13-yard line. We pulled out of that hole by forcing Taylor to fumble, and Danny Brabham, of Arkansas, recovered for us on the 12.

Griffing then surprised the Packers by sticking almost

exclusively to a running game on a 62-yard drive. Charlie Mitchell, of Washington, helped out with an 18-yard run, and Bill Thornton, of Nebraska, gained 16 on one play, but most of it was ground out on short-yardage plays.

The Packers finally held us on the 26, and on fourth and two, Jencks booted a 33-yard field goal to give us a 13-10 lead with just under 11 minutes left in the final period.

We clung to this lead through most of the last period, but it looked like the Packers might pull it out when Elijah Pitts broke loose for a 43-yard gain. Only a fine tackle on the 17-yard line by Kermit Alexander, of UCLA, saved the touchdown.

After an incomplete pass, Fred Miller, of LSU, and Brabham nailed Pitts for an eight-yard loss. On third and 18, Starr dropped back and tossed a screen pass to Taylor, but Bell read the play perfectly and dropped Jim for a six-yard loss. Pushed back to our 31, Kramer missed a 38-yard field goal which could have tied the score.

There was 4:15 left in the game when we took over on our 20, and I had a tough decision to make. Terry Baker and Sonny Gibbs, both outstanding quarterbacks, still had not been given a chance to play. What do you do? Do you take the risk and put a cold quarterback in at this stage or do you go back to VanderKelen, who looked so great in the first half?

I didn't like the idea of violating my rule of playing every man who has earned the right to get into the game, but I also felt that I had an obligation to the entire team and the fans.

I called Baker over, and he sensed what I was about to ask him. He was a big man about it. "Don't worry about me," he said

So with a chance to win if we could just keep possession of the ball, I sent Ron back into the game.

Thornton gained two and Mitchell picked up four, and we were faced with a third down and four from the 26.

As always, I had allowed my quarterbacks to call most of the plays, but this was a spot where I thought I should make the decision. I called a short down-and-out pass to Richter, just long enough for the first down.

Ron hit his target perfectly on the 31-yard line, and Richter would have been stopped there if Jesse Whittenton had played him instead of the ball. But Jesse was trying for the interception, and when he failed, Richter took off and wound up with a 74-yard touchdown to sew up the game for us. Quite honestly, I felt that some of the other Green Bay secondary were loafing on the play and might have stopped Richter. Instead of rushing over and heading for Richter as soon as the ball was in the air, they just stood and watched.

Although you always take a chance whenever you put the ball in the air, I thought this particular pass was as safe as you could call. It was a simple pattern to a tall, strong receiver and would be extremely difficult to stop.

When you're faced with a third and four situation in a spot like that, you don't even consider a running play against the tough Packer line and linebackers. I would hate to try making a living that way. Sure it could be done, but you would miss many more times than you would succeed. If we had failed to make this first down, we would have been forced to kick, and with three minutes left in the game, the Packers had plenty of time to tie or beat us.

Now, with a 20-10 lead, we had it all wrapped up, and the Green Bay touchdown with six seconds left in the game didn't mean a thing.

It was my greatest victory as a coach, and many consider the game the best of the All Star games ever played.

VanderKelen and Griffing mixed their plays beautifully. We not only gained 140 yards on the ground, but VanderKelen completed nine of 11 passes for 141 yards while Griffing hit on six out of ten for 142 yards.

Our front line allowed Taylor only 51 yards on 16 carries, and our secondary didn't give the Packers the long pass this time. We played good football all the way. We made them earn every yard they gained.

Participating in the College All Star game has always been an exciting experience for me, and I had the privilege of playing with both the All Stars and the pros before being invited to serve as coach of the All Stars.

George Halas

Professional football owes much of its current success to George S. Halas, who helped organize the National Football League in 1921.

He was the first to bring the modern T formation to the pros, the first to study motion pictures of the game, the first to hold daily practice sessions.

During the 39 years that he served as coach of the Chicago Bears, he compiled the enviable record of 321 regular season victories against 142 defeats and 31 ties. He is the all-time most winning coach in the pro or college ranks.

His Bears won world championships in 1921, 1933, 1940, 1941, 1946, and 1963. In only six of his 39 seasons did any of his teams fall below the .500 mark. Two of his teams had perfect seasons while seven lost only one game.

A member of the Pro Football Hall of Fame, Halas points with pride to the fact that there are more of his Chicago players in the Hall of Fame than any other team. These include: Red Grange, Sid Luckman, Paddy Driscoll, Bulldog Turner, Bronko Nagurski, Gale Sayers, George Connor, Bill Hewitt, Bill George, Joe Stydahar, George McAfee, Dan Fortman, Ed Healy, George Trafton, and Link Lyman.

Halas, a former University of Illinois football star, has been the owner of the Chicago Bears since he organized the team in

1921. He retired as coach after the 1967 season but still remains active in the front office operation of the team as chairman.

In 1970, he was elected the first president of the National Football Conference, a position which he still holds.

He was born in Chicago on February 2, 1895.

Chicago 73, Washington 0
1940 NFL CHAMPIONSHIP GAME

By George S. Halas

As head coach of the Chicago Bears for 40 years, I had many memorable games, but when you limit it to my most memorable, it can only be our 73-0 playoff victory over Sammy Baugh and the Washington Redskins for the 1940 world's professional championship.

A close second would have to be the 1934 title game which we lost, 30-13, to the New York Giants under quite unusual circumstances. I'll certainly never forget that contest, which became known as the "sneakers" or "rubber shoe" game.

It was played on December 9 under horrendous weather conditions. A regular nor'easter was blowing; the temperature was nine degrees and the Polo Grounds was covered with a sheet of ice.

Bronko Nagurski's touchdown and Jack Manders' field goal offset Ken Strong's field goal to give us a 10-3 lead at half time, but Coach Steve Owen outfitted the Giants in basketball shoes in the second half, and the sure footing enabled them to score four last-period touchdowns.

Ironically enough, I had remarked on the way out to the Polo Grounds that after all our careful preparations, we had overlooked one thing—tennis shoes. And that made the difference.

It ended an 18-game winning streak which still stands as a record in league play. The streak had started near the end of the

1933 season when we won our four last regularly scheduled games and then beat the Giants, 23-21, for the championship. In 1934, we won 13 in a row, including two victories over the Giants, before we lost to them in the playoffs.

We found little consolation in beating the Giants, 21-0, a month later in a post-season game in Los Angeles. Although we had defeated them three times, they were still the 1934 league champions.

I consider the 1934 Bears on par with my 1940 club which has been rated the best pro football team of all time by the National Academy of Sports Editors. In finishing the regular season undefeated, the '34 team led the league in rushing, total yards, and scoring. They would have repeated as world champions, too, if they had worn sneakers.

There were a number of reasons why I selected our 73-0 victory on December 8, 1940, in Washington over the Redskins as my most memorable one. Of course, the score was the most striking reason.

To me, it was the greatest team effort in my entire career as a coach. Everybody wanted to play, and when they got into the game, every player was at peak form. No changes in the lineup had any effect at all on the overall performance of the team.

All 33 players on the squad saw action. Sid Luckman played only the first half. Bernie Masterson, Bob Snyder, and Sollie Sherman alternated at quarterback in the second half, but it was impossible to hold the score down. Every man was in there to win and to contribute something to the winning. I can't recall any high scoring game where the distribution of touchdowns was so widespread. Ten different players scored our 11 touchdowns. Only Harry Clark scored twice.

The game resulted in the universal acceptance of the T formation which all teams now use. I well remember that Earle "Greasy" Neale, who was to become head coach of the Philadelphia Eagles in 1941, got the film of the game and charted every play, saying that any system good enough to score that many points was going to be good enough for him.

This game also avenged a 7-3 defeat at the hands of the

Redskins just three weeks earlier. We thought that we were going to win on the final play of that game when Luckman passed from the Redskin six-yard line to Bill Osmanski in the end zone. It was a perfect strike that bounced off Bill's chest. There was a good reason why Bill had been unable to catch the pass. His hands had been pinned to his side by Frank Filchock. The officials did not call interference despite our players' protests, and the game was over.

In post-game interviews, the Redskins called the Bears "cry-babies" while George Marshall, owner of the Redskins, made the tart observation that we were front runners and strictly a first-half ball club which folded when the going got tough.

The heart-breaking loss and the snide remarks combined to inspire the Bears to herculean efforts in preparing for the championship game. I don't think that the players needed any reminders, but on the Monday before the playoff, our dressing room walls were plastered with clippings detailing the Redskins' opinions of the Bears.

Hunk Anderson and Carl Brumbaugh were my only assistants in those days, so I brought in Clark Shaughnessy, head coach at Stanford, to give us a hand for the title game. Clark, who had taken the T formation to Stanford and had enjoyed a great season, was a wizard in analyzing game film. We ran and re-ran films of our loss to Washington. We determined why certain plays worked and why others failed. The players were shown their mistakes on film over and over again. Certain plays would be re-run 30 to 40 times at one sitting.

Each morning session would start with the showing of the film. Then, there was practice on the field, followed by chalk talks, lectures, written examinations on individual assignments, and more movies.

When we left Chicago for Washington by train, I never saw a squad of players so deadly serious. There was none of the card playing or joking or pranks or laughing that is part of the relaxation on a road trip. The players sat huddled in their seats, studying their notebooks.

Rarely have I used oratory to fire up a team before it takes the field for a game. In any event, it certainly was not necessary before this game. The squad was heated mentally to the maximum.

We reviewed our two offensive game plans just before the kickoff. Game plan No. 1 would be in effect if the Redskins used the same defense they had employed in our previous game. Our first four plays were designed to feel them out, but as it turned out, we found the answer after just two plays. They were using the same defense and game plan. No. 2 was never needed.

As for our defensive plans, we were thoroughly familiar with the Washington offense, and since we had held them to seven points in our last meeting, we were satisfied that we had them defensed very well.

Our main concern, of course, was Baugh. With his quick release—his ability to get the ball off so fast—there was no value in rushing him. Our defensive ends would drop back to cover the flat. This strategy proved especially effective in the third period when we intercepted three passes and ran them back for touchdowns. In all, we picked off eight of their passes.

We received the opening kickoff, and Luckman immediately called a "feeler" play to test the Redskins' defense. Ken Kavanaugh, our left end, was placed 18 yards out on the flank, and the Washington right halfback followed him out. Ray Nolting, at left half, was sent in motion to the right, and the Redskins' linebacker trailed him.

That was all Luckman had to see. The Redskin defense had not changed. George McAfee took a short pitch from Luckman and bolted between right guard and tackle for eight yards.

Then, on the next play, Kavanaugh again went wide, but McAfee went in motion to his left. Luckman made a reverse pivot and handed the ball to Osmanski on a run to the spread side. I remember later that Sid said: "Bill was really driving when I handed off. I knew he was going some place in a hurry."

That "some place" was 68 yards to a touchdown.

Actually, this play did not go according to plan. It originally called for a straight slant off left tackle, but when McAfee's block had not flattened the Redskin right end, Osmanski was afraid that

Coach GEORGE ALLEN and his three sons celebrate a Washington Redskin victory.

Oakland Coach, JOHN MADDEN, left, and Managing General Partner, AL DAVIS, accept the Vince Lombardi Super Bowl trophy

BART STARR, one of the greatest quarterbacks of all time, now head coach and general manager of the Green Bay Packers

Quarterback JOE NAMATH and former New York Jet Coach WEEB EWBANK

The late VINCE LOMBARDI, being carried off the field by Jerry Kramer (64) and Green Bay team-mates.

GEORGE HALAS, one of the founders of the NFL and former coach of the
Chicago Bears, with **RAYMOND BERRY (82)** and Terry Barr (41) during
the 1964 Pro Bowl game.

Ex-Cleveland and Cincinnati Coach PAUL BROWN, left, with Miami Coach
DON SHULA.

Coach HANK STRAM, who led Kansas City to a Super Bowl victory, now
rebuilding the New Orleans Saints.

SID GILLMAN, when head coach of the San Diego Chargers.

The late DON MCCAFFERTY looks on as JOHNNY UNITAS accepts the
Super Bowl trophy for the Baltimore Colts.

Head Coach TED MARCHIBRODA of the Baltimore Colts.

CHUCK FAIRBANKS, New England Patriots coach, with STEVE BURKS and
RANDY VATAHA.

Hall of Famer OTTO GRAHAM, now
Captain Graham of the U.S. Coast Guard
Academy.

The late EARLE "GREASY" NEALE,
former Philadelphia coach.

Dallas Coach TOM LANDRY on the sidelines with GOLDEN RICHARDS and
ROGER STAUBACH.

the end would reach out and grab him so he made a dip towards the line and then ran wide around the end. Bill streaked away as George Musso blocked out the up-man in the secondary. Near the Redskin 35, Ed Justice and Jimmy Johnston started to close in on Bill, but neither saw George Wilson, who had cut across fast from his right end position.

As Justice started to tackle Osmanski, Wilson hit him with such force that the impact sent him into Johnston. Two men on one block! Osmanski went the rest of the way all by himself, and we had our first score after only 55 seconds.

The Redskins came roaring back. Max Krause took the kickoff on his four and ran it back 56 yards before Osmanski tackled him on our 40 and prevented him from going all the way. Baugh moved the Redskins to the 25, but our defense held and Bob Masterson's 32-yard field-goal attempt failed.

We took over on our 20, and in 17 plays we went 80 yards, with Luckman sneaking over from the one-foot line for our second touchdown. Sid remained on the ground all the way during this drive. Our running game was doing the job, and wise quarterback that he was, Sid stayed with what was working.

A few minutes later, we took a 21-0 lead when Joe Maniaci raced 42 yards on a standard fullback-lateral play.

We missed two scoring opportunities in the second quarter, once when Ray McLean fumbled on the Redskins' 11 on a first-down play and later, when Phil Martinovich failed on a 30-yard field goal attempt.

Finally, near the end of the period, we were able to get on the scoreboard again. After Nolting intercepted a Filchock pass on our 34 and ran it back ten yards, we moved to the Redskins' 30 on six ground plays. Then, on one of the few times we passed all day, Luckman hit Kavanaugh with a perfect toss in the corner of the end zone over the heads of Filchock and Andy Farkas.

The Redskins' most serious scoring threat came as time was running out in the half when they went 75 yards on eight pass plays to within one yard of our goal line. But Osmanski intercepted Baugh's pass on the final play of the half.

What do you tell a team in the dressing room at half-time

when it has performed so magnificently and is leading 28-0? I simply told them: "Don't forget . . . the Redskins called us a first-half team apt to fold in the second half   . don't forget that!"

The players let out a roar which more than convinced me of their readiness for the second half.

On the second play of the third period, Baugh's pass in the flat was intercepted by Hampton Pool, who ran it back 15 yards for the touchdown. It was our defensive plan against Baugh working to perfection.

Then, trailing 35-0, Baugh became desperate. On fourth and 20 from his own 34, he attempted a long pass which was incomplete. We took over deep in Redskin territory.

Nolting picked up 11 yards and then, on a quick opening play, he went over tackle, broke into the open, side-stepped Baugh and scored on a 23-yard run. Nolting was superb on these quick openers, and there hasn't been anyone better to this day.

Two more pass interceptions gave us a 54-0 lead by the time the third period ended. McAfee made a shoe string catch of a pass by Roy Zimmerman and went 34 yards, and Clyde Turner ran 21 yards after picking off another Zimmerman toss.

With a rookie quarterback, Sollie Sherman, running the team, we drove 58 yards on nine running plays for our ninth touchdown of the game. Harry Clark went the final 44 yards on a double reverse, a play that worked far more successfully than expected. But it was an afternoon when we could do nothing wrong.

In just a few minutes, the parade of touchdowns continued. A snap from center got away from Filchock, and Turner recovered for us on the Redskins' two. After Gary Famiglietti scored, the referee came over and asked us not to attempt the extra point with a kick. It seemed that we had kicked so many balls into the stands that only practice balls were left. So instead of trying the conversion by place-kicking, we passed and Sherman's completion to Maniaci made it 67-0, a new league record.

On the second play after the kick-off, Maniaci intercepted a long Filchock pass—our eighth interception of the game—and returned 21 yards to the Redskins' 42. With Snyder now in at quarterback, we scored on 11 plays, Clark getting our eleventh and final touchdown on a plunge from the one.

The massacre was over. It had been impossible to hold the score down. The fierce competitive desires of the entire squad had been too great. Every element of offensive and defensive play had contributed to this historic game.

Tom Landry

Tom Landry, the only coach the Dallas Cowboys have had since they became an expansion team in 1960, ranks second as the most winning active coach in the NFL and sixth among the all-time most winning coaches.

He has accomplished this great record by leading the Cowboys to a 137-93-6 mark during his 17 years as their head coach.

This record is all the more amazing in view of the fact that Dallas was 25-53-4 during their first six years in the NFL, but once Landry had developed his organization, their record since 1966 has been 112-40-2, with 10 playoff appearances in 11 years, three National Football Conference titles, and one Super Bowl victory.

Born in Mission, Texas, on September 11, 1924, Landry was an all-regional fullback at his local high school before enrolling in the University of Texas.

He left school after one semester to join the Air Force during World War II and flew 30 B-17 missions over Germany.

Landry returned to the University of Texas at the end of the war, was All-Southwest Conference back in his junior year and co-captained the team his senior year.

He played with the New York Yankees in the All-America Conference in 1949 and joined the New York Giants the following year. He was the key to the famed Giants' umbrella defense through 1955 and served as player-coach during his final two seasons with the Giants. In 1954, he was accorded All-Pro honors.

He remained with the Giants as a defensive coach through the 1959 season when he was named to head the Dallas Cowboys.

Dallas 24, Miami 3
1972 SUPER BOWL VI

By Tom Landry

Back in 1960, the first season in the National Football League for the Dallas Cowboys, our expansion team lost 11 games, tied one, and failed to win a single game. It was a painful experience, but no one connected with the Dallas organization was discouraged.

We had four more losing seasons until 1965 when we broke even in 14 games to finish second in the Eastern Division, and the following year, we finally put it all together to win the Division title.

That championship in 1966 was the start of our becoming the perennial Division champions, but it was also the beginning of an unpleasant situation. We had to live under the shadow of being called the team that could not win the big one.

In 1966, we lost the NFL title to Green Bay, 34-27, in a free scoring game that we almost won, and the next year, we lost to the Packers, 21-17, in a game considered by many as one of the greatest pro games ever played. The next two years, we lost to Cleveland in the playoffs, and in 1970, when we won our first NFL championship, we lost Super Bowl V to Baltimore, 16-13, on a field goal in the final seconds.

The most disappointing of all these defeats was our loss to Green Bay, 21-17, on Bart Starr's quarterback sneak as time was running out. I thought that we had a better team, and when we erased a 14-0 deficit to lead, 17-14, going into the closing minutes, only to lose, you can well imagine our frustration.

It's bad enough to lose a championship or playoff game, but when you are tagged as a team that never wins the big one, you get concerned because you know the effect that all this has on your players.

I personally never became too upset because I knew that we had a fine, solid ball team, and I was confident that eventually we would win the Super Bowl which is the ultimate goal in our profession.

So, beating Miami, 24-3, in Super Bowl VI in New Orleans on January 16, 1972, had to be my greatest game as a pro coach. It was a great accomplishment for the Cowboys, who had started as the worst team in the NFL and now were the world's champions.

None of this could have happened without a superb Dallas organization. You have to start with stability at the top. You need an owner who won't be influenced by the fans or the press or any of the other pressures placed upon a person who owns a franchise. The Cowboys happen to be blessed with Clint Murchison, who believes that when you put a man in a position as coach, you let him go on his own, and you stick by him until he proves himself.

That's the main reason that we were able to become so successful. We have a stable organization. Tex Schramm has been president, and I have been coach of the Cowboys all these years because in Clint Murchison, we have a man on top who doesn't panic when the going gets tough.

In reaching the Super Bowl for the second year in a row, we were a very confident and poised team. Although Miami had whipped the defending champion Baltimore Colts, 21-0, for the AFC title, we felt that the experience of our first appearance in this classic the year before would be helpful. And after all the abuse and heartaches of the past, the team was mentally tough.

What had been distractions the year before did not bother us this time. We knew what was coming, and it did not disturb us. There's a certain aura about the Super Bowl. When you spend so many years trying to get into the biggest of all games and finally get there, it almost seems unreal and it has a tremendous effect on you. That's been proven by the records which show that a team playing in the Super Bowl for the first time rarely beats a team that has been there before.

We were more relaxed for our second trip to the Super Bowl and were able to plan our daily schedule more effectively. After tough playoff games against Minnesota and San Francisco, the players needed some rest so with an extra week available, we were able to give them several days off. Later in the week, we practiced, mainly for the purpose of tuning up.

In New Orleans, once picture day was out of the way on Monday, we were able to settle down to our normal schedule of practices.

We had started formulating our game plans during the first week, and once they were completed and presented to the players, we constantly reviewed them. We went over every detail so many times that the players were well prepared when game time rolled around.

Miami was an extremely well-balanced team, and this was actually the beginning of some great Dolphin teams. They had great weapons, and we were fortunate enough to have an advantage because of our experience.

Their defense had allowed only 174 points during the regular season and was especially impressive in shutting out Baltimore in the AFC championship game.

Our strongest asset offensively was our running game, but in order to make it work, we knew that we had to handle Miami's veteran middle linebacker, Nick Buoniconti. He was the key to their defense, and if we could push him by the hole or misdirect him, our running game would be successful.

We did not want Roger Staubach to pass any more than was absolutely necessary.

Defensively, we had the dual task of containing Paul Warfield and Larry Csonka. We would double-team Warfield as much as possible, keep him off-balance, and prevent him from making the big, easy play. From time to time, we'd cover him man-to-man so that Miami would never know for sure what our coverage would be.

Miami's running game had been very successful all year, and it wasn't too difficult to predict where they were going to run. Since our defense at Dallas is geared to the running game, we were determined to control Csonka at his point of attack.

In the dressing room before the game, we just touched base with our quarterbacks and some other players, mainly to see what their pulse was at that time. We had covered everything so many times during the week that there was no need for any review. We just asked if there were any questions.

I didn't give them any pep talk before the game. Although I believe that emotion is very important, false emotion is never successful. Emotion is built over a period of time, not in one day or even one week. I don't think that you can get a team up for a game by giving them a "Win one for the Gipper" pep talk before the kickoff.

I tried doing that once when I felt the players weren't ready for a game. They charged out of the dressing room and looked like a million bucks the first two minutes, scoring immediately. But then we were beaten, 34-7.

If a team isn't ready, nothing is going to get them up. Emotion comes from preparation and planning. You must remember that emotion can cover up inadequacies, and in the end can get in the way of performance.

You cannot keep a team emotionally high over an entire season or even over a few games. You win championships by not having highly emotional games. Whenever you do, the chances are that you'll be flat the next week.

People get the impression that I am unemotional because they see me concentrating so hard on what I'm doing on the sidelines. During a game, you cannot be emotional and still concentrate on your job. Our system at Dallas is a complicated one. Other teams have simpler concepts, and their coaches can show more emotion.

Because of our complicated offense and defense, I have to be thinking a couple of plays ahead at all times. It's important to remain calm and be able to make split-second judgments.

We send in plays for both our offense and defense, and that should not be taken as a lack of confidence in either our quarterback or defensive leader. They could call plays as well as anybody, but we call the plays because it gives us more control of the game. By knowing what plays are coming up, we can better determine how the opposition is reacting.

We have confidence in our ability to call the plays, and that is one of the most important qualities that you can really have in the coaching business. Confidence is contagious, and if you can transmit this aura to your players, it can bring the ultimate success.

We were a confident Dallas team when we kicked off to Miami. Early in the first quarter, Csonka fumbled for the first time that entire season and Chuck Howley recovered for us on our 48. Duane Thomas picked up two yards, Roger Staubach ran for gains of five and four yards on consecutive plays for a first down on the Miami 41.

Neither of Staubach's runs were planned plays. He was supposed to pass both times but ran on his own initiative. It's very seldom that we ever call a running play for Roger. Except for an occasional quarterback draw play, he runs spontaneously, and although his ability as a runner has worried many opponents, we prefer delegating our running game to our other backs. That way Roger will be able to be with us many more seasons.

We moved the ball very well on this drive, but on fourth and goal from the two, we were forced to settle for a field goal by Mike Clark.

We controlled the ball for more than eight minutes on that drive, and Miami had the opportunity to run only eight plays during the first quarter.

Midway in the second quarter, we started a drive on our own 24 and went 76 yards in 11 plays for our first touchdown. It was another important time-consuming drive that ate up six and a half minutes on the clock.

Seven of the plays were on the ground which was all part of

115

our game plan. We did not want to put the ball in the air too much against Miami's 53 defense which gave them extra coverage against our receivers. We wanted to run every opportunity that we had, forcing them to bring up more people to try to stop our running game, and then hit them with a pass.

A Staubach-to-Lance Alworth pass for 21 yards in the midst of our ground attack was typical of our strategy. Climaxing the drive was a seven-yard pass to Alworth, a perfect toss by Staubach in the corner of the end zone, set up by runs of 13, 7, and 5 by Calvin Hill on the three previous plays.

With 1:15 left in the half, we had a 10-0 lead, and our job was to make certain that Miami didn't score with so little time left. If Miami could score and get back into the ball game, they would be leaving the field with a great deal of confidence. We had to prevent the deep pass.

Mercury Morris returned the kickoff to his own 32. Bob Griese passed to Warfield for five and to Jim Kiick for 11. Those short passes weren't bothering us, and we were now down to 22 seconds. Still enough time for a passer like Griese to get some points on the board, and he put Miami within field goal range by completing a 23-yard pass to Warfield on our 24.

With only eight seconds left, Garo Yepremian was rushed into the game to try a 31-yard field goal. It was good, cutting our lead to 10-3 at the half.

We had not been able to prevent Miami from scoring, and although they were able to leave the field with a great deal of enthusiasm, our team was not down. They were so experienced and so tough that hardly anything would have shaken them. I don't think that it would have bothered them if they had fallen behind at the half.

This was a determined, confident team.

Even though we led by only seven points, we had completely dominated the first half, and our game plan was working well. We had kept the ball on the ground in 22 plays for 124 yards and completed eight of 13 passes for 72 yards. Csonka had been held to 15 yards, and Griese's longest completion had been a 23-yard pass to Warfield, who was so well-covered that he could make only two receptions.

We had proven that we could move the ball against the tough Miami defense, and I was sure that we would be able to score again. If we could control the third quarter, we could win the game. The third quarter is most often the time when you win or lose a game. We wanted to make sure that we didn't make any mistakes in the third quarter as we had the year before when a Duane Thomas fumble stopped a great drive that might have given us the Super Bowl victory a year earlier.

We wanted to put the pressure on Miami in the third quarter and not let them get back into the ball game.

After Thomas returned the second half kickoff 23 yards to our 29, we did just that, moving 71 yards in just eight plays. Using pitch-outs and sweeps along with a reverse, Staubach passed only once during this drive and that was on a third and three situation when he hit Hill for 12 yards.

The two other big plays in setting up the touchdown was a 23-yard run off the right side by Thomas and a 16-yard reverse by Bob Hayes. On second and goal from the three, Thomas took a pitch-out and powered his way around left end for the score. Clark's extra point gave us a 17-3 lead.

It also gave us the momentum we wanted and was probably the decisive drive of the game. Miami had to be frustrated. They had not been able to do much against us during the first half, and here we came right out in the third quarter and scored immediately. We never looked better than we did on that drive. Our blocking was as crisp as it had ever been, and we had been able to follow our game plan by keeping the ball on the ground.

We continued to dominate the rest of the period. Miami had control of the ball for only eight plays and was unable to make a single first down. A combination of a strong rush against Griese and excellent coverage in our secondary prevented any pass completion in four attempts. Csonka was stopped with just four yards in two carries.

Early in the final period, Howley picked off a pass at midfield by stepping in front of the intended receiver, Kiick, and ran the ball back 41 yards to the Miami nine. He almost went all the way. Two plays later, Staubach passed seven yards to Mike Ditka, our tight end, in the end zone, and Clark kicked the extra point to give us a 24-3 lead.

With a 21-point lead and 11:25 left in the game, you feel pretty confident, but you know from past experience that you can't take anything for granted. We had complete control of the game up to this point, but we still had to worry about the explosive Miami offense with Griese, Warfield, and Csonka.

With 8:33 left, Griese lost the ball on a fumble on our 16-yard line to stop their only threat of the second half, and you could then feel an air of jubilation among the players on the sidelines.

We almost scored again on an 80-yard drive, but no one was upset when Hill fumbled the ball away on the Miami one-yard line. It was all over, and the team that couldn't win the big one had won the biggest one of all.

In winning, we had been able to follow our game plan all the way. We took the big play away from Warfield, whose four receptions totalled only 39 yards. Csonka was held to 40 yards, with half of that amount coming in the final period.

We set a Super Bowl record with 252 yards on the ground, and that made our passing game effective whenever we wanted to go to the air. Staubach was able to complete 12 of 19 passes.

We controlled the ball on 69 offensive plays as compared to 44 for Miami.

The victory was a great relief for all of us, and it was accomplished because of the experiences we had gone through as a team during the five previous seasons.

We won because we had a squad of players who were competitive and had the desire to win. They had the ability to divert some of their drive for self-acclaim to team achievement.

You have prima donnas on your hands when you have players who don't have the ability to sacrifice some of their own self-glory for the benefit of the team. You've got to be a team man to play football and at the same time possess that individual drive that makes you great. If you can't make the adjustment to do what is best for the team, you don't stay around very long. That's why you see talented players drift from team to team.

Our team also displayed great character by overcoming adversity. If we had not been through so much adversity, we might never have developed the character needed to become a championship team.

Duane Thomas, of course, had been a major problem for us. He had been traded to New England but had trouble there and wound up back with us.

We're pretty strict as far as discipline is concerned, and although it's important to treat everyone the same, you have to be flexible and make exceptions as long as the rest of the squad goes along with you. We took Thomas back and made special concessions to him as far as our rules were concerned only because the team was willing to accept it.

It was far from a happy or ideal situation, but once again, I must point out that this was a team with great character, and without this trait, we just as easily could have been 3 and 11 that year instead of 11 and 3 and Super Bowl champions.

IX

John Madden

When John Madden was a rookie offensive tackle with the Philadelphia Eagles in 1959, his career as a pro player came to an abrupt halt when surgery was required on an injured knee.

That injury forced him to report to the training room for treatment each morning and enabled him to spend considerable time with Norm Van Brocklin, the Eagles quarterback who would be there early to study game films.

Madden also learned more from Van Brocklin about the overall game instead of just his individual assignments as a player, and this eventually led to his determination to become a coach.

He started as an assistant at Hanock Junior College in Santa Maria, Cal., where he spent four years, the last two as head coach. He moved on to San Diego State and won considerable acclaim as defensive coordinator in 1964 when the Aztecs were ranked No. 1 among small colleges.

In 1967, Madden became linebacker coach for Oakland, and two years later, at age 32, he became head coach of the Raiders. His team had a 12-1-1 record that first year to earn him Coach of the Year honors and start him on a string of highly successful seasons.

During his eight years as head of the Raiders, his teams have won 83 regular season games and have never lost more than four games in any one season. Only once during those years has Oakland failed to win the AFC Western Division title.

His Super Bowl XI championship team took a ten-game winning streak into the playoffs where they added three more wins. In 1971 and 1974, his teams had nine-game winning streaks.

Madden served as head coach of the AFC team in the Pro Bowl in 1970, 1973, 1974, and 1975.

He was born in Austin, Minn., April 10, 1936, and was an all-conference tackle at California Polytechnic College.

Oakland 32, Minnesota 14

1977 SUPER BOWL XI

By John Madden

In 1973, Oakland was beaten in the American Football Conference championship game by Miami, 27-10. In 1974, we lost the AFC title to Pittsburgh, 24-13. Then in 1975, the Raiders again were defeated by Pittsburgh, 16-10, in the title game.

For three consecutive years, Oakland had a chance to go to the Super Bowl, and each time failed to make it. To get so close and then not make it to the biggest of all games was disappointing, to say the least, but it was never frustrating. In each of those years, the team that beat us went on to win the Super Bowl so there was the consolation of losing to the world's champions.

During those three years and others that preceded them, Oakland had won many exciting games. Any number of times, games were decided in the closing seconds, and it was exhilarating being able to leave the field a winner when you had appeared doomed to be beaten.

There were many moments like these, but none of them can compare to the feeling when you win the Super Bowl. Accomplishing this feat with a team that was forced to overcome many adverse situations all season has made Super Bowl XI my greatest game.

Playing in the Super Bowl is what pro football is all about. This is the ultimate. It's between the two best teams. Make no mistake. You've got to be great to get that far.

Actually, getting into the playoffs is a major accomplishment in itself. You are the only one of eight teams from among 28 teams that started the season. Many of these 28 teams are outstanding, yet only the eight best make it to the playoffs. One week later, only four teams are left, and they do battle for the right to meet in the Super Bowl.

When Oakland finally made it to Super Bowl XI on January 9, 1977, against Minnesota, it was only part of the goal that had eluded us so long. Now, the team wanted to make sure that it reached the pinnacle by taking the Vince Lombardi Trophy home.

Preparation for Oakland's appearance in the Super Bowl actually started several years earlier. Having been selected as coach of the AFC team gave us the opportunity to talk with players who had just finished playing in the Super Bowl.

These players talked about things that had bothered them in the handling of arrangements for the game, and they also told about the distractions they encountered the week of the game.

Ticket allocation and distribution always seemed to be a problem so the first thing was to give the players their tickets and allow them plenty of time to distribute them. Now that's just a little thing, but it can create problems if not handled properly.

Then, it was decided that each player, married or single, could select one person for whom the Raiders would provide transportation and a room for the game. At the Pro Bowl, some of the single players had complained that they had been discriminated against by their teams at the Super Bowl because married players were able to take their wives, and they could not take anyone.

Other players had complained about the distractions caused early in the week by the large number of new media personnel. Our players were told that the news conferences on three of the days, lasting no more than one hour, was all part of Super Bowl week, and by cooperating with the media during the set times, they would not be bothered by the media the rest of the day.

The players weren't going to concentrate on football 24-

hours a day anyway, so they should not look at these meetings with the press as a distraction. Enough time would be set aside for them to concentrate on the game.

Another thing that helped the players was to turn off the telephones in their rooms at a certain hour so that they would not be disturbed by curious fans. The operators were instructed to take messages during those hours when the phone was turned off so the players could return whatever calls they felt were important.

There were other things that former participants in the Super Bowl found objectionable, but our squad was told that these were all part of the game, and as long as they had to do it, they might as well enjoy it.

Although some had complained that the Super Bowl should be played the week following the championship game, the extra week is needed. For one thing, it gave us time to relax and enjoy the championship victory over Pittsburgh. Players with bumps and bruises had additional time to get into perfect condition. All the little things like ticket distribution to the players can be done with a minimum of confusion.

It gave our coaching staff time to break down the films of the last three Minnesota games which they had sent us in exchange for ours, and it gave the players ample time to view these films.

During the first week, our coaching staff worked on our game plan, but it was not to be presented to the players until the following week.

During the first week, the players viewed the films solely to get acquainted with the Minnesota personnel, most of whom were strangers to us. The film had been broken down into offense, defense, and special teams. We talked about who they were and what they did, but we did not talk about what we planned to do.

Once the team arrived at Newport Beach, Oakland's headquarters for the week, a normal, day-to-day schedule was followed. They received the defensive game plan on Wednesday, offensive plan on Thursday, and special team plan on Friday.

Even though there was an extra week, it wasn't best to give them the game plans too early and then spend too much time reviewing it. That could be boring to the players.

Offensively, it was important not to get into any set pattern since Minnesota, a very experienced team, played very well against a set offense.

We wanted to get them in a position where they didn't know on a given down whether we were going to run or pass. We wanted to run and pass on first down; run and pass on second down; run and pass on third down; run and pass on long yardage situations; run and pass on short yardage.

We did not go into great detail on these plans with the entire team, just with our quarterbacks.

In Kenny Stabler, Oakland is blessed with a truly brilliant quarterback. Not only is he a great passer and leader but he has the ability to absorb an unlimited amount of information, store it away, and then use it at the right time. We gave him information every day and discussed the Minnesota films with him.

He has such a great feeling for the game that he is allowed to call his own plays, and nobody could have called a better game than he did against Minnesota.

Defensively, you had to eliminate the big play—the long gain. Watching the Minnesota film, it was apparent that they were dangerous, with at least four players capable of making the big play. There was Chuck Foreman, who could take a five-yard pass over the middle and turn it into an 80-yard play. Brent McClanahan could take a screen pass and do the same thing. Sammy White and Ahmad Rashad could burn you with the bomb.

If they completed a short pass, we had to make sure that they were tackled on the spot. White and Rashad must not be allowed to get even a half-step lead on any of our defenders. And as much pressure as possible had to be placed on Fran Tarkenton, whose passing is almost impossible to stop if you give him enough time.

Minnesota's ability to block punts and field goal attempts was no secret, but we planned nothing special. Having worked all year on giving our kickers adequate protection, we did not anticipate any problem.

Ray Guy, our punter, had never had a kick blocked since he joined our team as a No. 1 draft choice.

You feel a bit more secure when you have a punter like Guy on your team. He is a constant help to your defense by giving the opposition poor field position, and he enables us to gamble on offense, confident that he will kick us out of trouble if we fail to make the first down deep in our own territory.

As always, a great deal of time was spent with our special teams. You can play very well on offense and very well on defense, but many of your games would not be won without great performance from your special team. All too often you need them to give you good field position or to place the opposition in bad field position.

Originally, we had planned to stay at the Marriott Hotel in Newport Beach until it was time to leave for the game on Sunday morning, but when it was learned that it would take at least an hour and possibly longer to get to the Rose Bowl in Pasadena, plans were made to spend Saturday night at the Los Angeles Hilton.

The team had dinner together at 6 p.m. and then a bus was available to take players to a movie. Very few decided to go. Most of the players just stayed in their room and watched TV.

As before every game, there was a meeting with our quarterbacks at 7:30 to review our game plan.

After a team breakfast at 8:30 Sunday morning, there was a meeting for about 10 minutes, mainly to review our special team plans.

The team was scheduled to leave the hotel at 10 o'clock, based on a timing of 20 minutes to get to the Rose Bowl, but I was afraid that there might be delays from heavy traffic so we decided to leave at 9:45. With a police escort on the ground and a helicopter checking the roads ahead, the team arrived at the stadium in just 18 minutes. It was a relief to be settled in our locker room without having to fight any crowds.

Before the game, I simply told the players that it was all going to boil down to execution. We had to go out there and block and tackle.

Kickoff returns and kickoff coverages were discussed, and then the team said a short prayer.

No need to get into the obvious—that this was a big game. They all knew that. We were ready to play. I knew it, and they knew it. Motivation must come naturally. It starts with the player and is reinforced by the coach. Motivation through gimmicks just won't work. If you try to say something that doesn't come from within or try to be someone who is not really you, it doesn't mean a thing.

If ever there was a situation when players needed no motivation from a coach, this was it.

The team had overcome one adversity after another to get to the Super Bowl. It all started late in our training season when three defensive linemen, Art Thoms, Horace Jones, and Kelvin Korver, and running back, Marv Hubbard, were injured.

Losing three top defensive players just before the season was ready to start puts you in a bad hole, and we were forced to go to a three-man line. Otis Sistrunk was moved from tackle to right end, Dave Rowe was inserted in the middle guard position, and Charles Philyaw, a rookie, was used at left end. There wasn't much time to work with this new set-up, and it meant extra effort from all concerned.

Then, in the season opener against Pittsburgh, we were accused of being unnecessarily rough as a result of a defensive play by George Atkinson against Lynn Swann. The charges were totally unfair, but the controversy never seemed to stop, and we had to live under that cloud all season.

Near the end of the season before a game crucial to Cincinnati's playoff chances, there was endless talk about the fact that Oakland would lose to the Bengals in order to eliminate Pittsburgh so that we would not be forced to meet a stronger Steelers' team in the playoffs.

We settled that issue by beating Cincinnati decisively. But going into the playoffs against New England, the talk still continued about our team being unnecessarily rough. We trailed New England by 11 points in the last period, but two touchdowns, the final one with just 10 seconds to play, gave us a 24-21 victory.

Now it was Pittsburgh again for the Conference championship and the right to play in the Super Bowl. It shaped up as an excellent game between two outstanding teams, but once again, all the talk was about the rough tactics of our team. We played our usual hard-hitting but clean game, and whipped the Steelers, 24-7.

Many teams might have folded with all these problems, but perhaps these adverse situations helped play a part in molding us into Super Bowl champions.

In any event, I had a great feeling of confidence as we got ready to receive the opening kickoff. It was a confidence that had been building up all week.

We moved the ball well on the opening series and in eight plays were on Minnesota's 11-yard line. Errol Mann's try for a field goal from that point hit the left upright, and we failed to score. Mann had hit the ball well enough, and it was just a matter of inches that kept us from taking an early lead.

Late in the first period, when we were forced to punt from our 34, Fred McNeill came from the outside, made a great effort and blocked Guy's kick. McNeill recovered the ball, and Guy's tackle on the three-yard line kept him from going in for the touchdown.

My first thought was to be thankful that Guy had been able to get back quick enough to prevent the touchdown.

It never entered my mind that Minnesota was certain to come away with at least three points. I was concentrating on having our defense stop their first shot. When you're in a hole like this, you worry about one play at a time.

Foreman hit right tackle and was stopped by Philyaw after gaining only one yard. McClanahan went up the middle, but Phil Villapiano, one of our linebackers, had diagnosed the play, moved in quickly, and hit him so hard that it jarred the ball loose. Willie Hall recovered for us on the three.

Quite a few reported that this was one of the turning points if not the major turning point of the game, but I didn't feel that way. We had moved the ball so well in the first period, being able to do exactly what we had planned, that I felt that even if Minnesota had put seven points on the board first, we would have been able to beat them.

We took the ball on our three-yard line, and our first objective was to get the ball away from the goal line as quickly as possible. We inserted three tight ends for a couple of power shots, and on third and seven, Clarence Davis sped around left end and down the sidelines for a 35-yard gain. Gene Upshaw, pulling from his left guard position, made a key block that sprung Davis loose, and we no longer had our backs against the wall. It was a big play for us. Instead of being pinned down, we had good field position on our 41, and we could return to our normal offense.

We moved down to the Minnesota seven but were forced to settle for a 24-yard field goal by Mann after 48 seconds of the second period.

The next time that we got the ball, we went 64 yards on ten plays for our first touchdown and a 10-0 lead.

A leaping catch by Fred Biletnikoff of a Stabler pass gave us a first down on the Minnesota one-yard line, and we sent Henry Lawrence into the game to become our third tight end, along with Dave Casper and Warren Bankston.

We faked a run to try to draw in their secondary, and since we were so close to the goal line and were using three tight ends, they fell for it. Stabler faked the hand-off, dropped back quickly, and found Casper all alone in the end zone.

We had used play action passes all season, but this was the first time we had called it from this particular formation with three tight ends, and it could not have worked better.

A few minutes later, we were on the Minnesota 35, thanks to a nifty 25-yard punt return by Neal Colzie. Three running plays moved the ball to the 18, and on first down, with Minnesota expecting another running play, Stabler passed 17 yards to Biletnikoff who made a spectacular diving catch just short of the goal line. Kenny intentionally threw the ball low to keep cornerback Nate Wright from breaking up the play.

It was a simple post pattern, nothing different from what we had used all season. All this starts with our pass protection. Our line gives Kenny ample time to set up and spot his man. Fred makes a quick inside move, and with the best pair of hands in football, he pulls in the ball while falling to the ground. Fred has made so many almost impossible catches for us through the years that it's almost routine for him.

Banaszak went over right tackle for the touchdown; Mann missed the extra point and at 11:27 of the second period, we led, 16-0.

We took that lead into the locker room at half time along with some very impressive statistics. We had compiled 16 first downs to four for Minnesota. We converted on seven of 12 third downs while they were one for six. We had 288 total yards to their 86. Stabler had completed ten of 15 passes while Tarkenton was only five for 12. We had a well-balanced attack with 166 yards rushing and 122 yards passing.

Statistics can sometimes be misleading, but in this case they weren't. We had succeeded in the first half in doing exactly what we had set out to do. We were running when they expected us to pass, and we were passing when they looked for the run. Defensively, we had kept them from making the big play.

The half-time intermission was 22 minutes instead of the usual 15, and that time was spent reviewing what we had done and what they had done. Then, we discussed what to anticipate from them in the second half, and what we planned to do.

We wanted to keep putting the pressure on them defensively. We did not want to sit on a 16-point lead or to play as though we had the game in the bag. We wanted to play an aggressive game, to produce yardage and more points.

I didn't have to tell the players not to get over confident because we had a 16-0 lead. They had studied the films and knew Minnesota was an explosive team. They realized that with players like Tarkenton, Foreman, White, and Rashad, Minnesota had the ability to score at any time.

We just had 30 minutes left between us and the world's championship—everything that we had fought for all season—and we sure as heck weren't going to let it escape now.

One of the best things about the game in the second half was that we passed on first down the very first time we got the ball. That set the tempo for us the rest of the way. Had we tried three running plays and then had to punt, it might have set a different pattern.

Throwing on first down was Kenny's call. I had not specifically told him to throw on first down on the first series. We had discussed during the half that this was the sort of thing we wanted to do, but I didn't tell him when he should call that type of play.

Mann kicked a 40-yard field goal to make it 19-0 at 9:44 of the third period, and Minnesota finally scored with 35 seconds left in the period, with Tarkenton climaxing a 58-yard drive with an eight-yard pass to Sammy White in the end zone.

I wasn't worried about the possibility that the momentum was now changing. If we stayed consistent, continued to play special teams the way we were and move the ball as we had, we would score again, and that was all we needed.

Minnesota was moving the ball well early in the fourth quarter and had a third and three on our 37 when Ted Hendricks put tremendous pressure on Tarkenton, forcing him to overthrow Foreman. Willie Hall intercepted on our 30 and ran the ball back 16 yards.

On third and six from mid-field, Kenny spotted Biletnikoff wide open on the 35 in the middle of Minnesota's zone. Fred made an easy catch and ran all the way back to the two-yard line before he was stopped by Bryant. Banaszak again went over right tackle for the touchdown, and Mann's extra point made it 26-7, with 7:29 left to play.

Our final score came two minutes later when Willie Brown picked off a Tarkenton pass on our 25 and sped down the sidelines untouched. Mann's conversion try was wide, but with 5:33 left, we were ahead, 32-7, and the rest of the game didn't matter.

I didn't even see the final Minnesota touchdown that made it 32-14 in the closing seconds. The squad had swarmed around me, and it wasn't until later that I learned that the score had come on an eight-yard pass from Bob Lee to Stu Voigt.

The players picked me up to carry me off the field, and someone said that this was the hardest task they had all day.

It may have been a clever remark, but it wasn't quite true. Minnesota was a great ball club. They had to be great to get where they were. We had to work plenty hard to beat them, and the score didn't indicate the true strength of the Minnesota team.

The media and the fans will keep saying that Bud Grant and Minnesota never win the big ones. That's unfair. They've won plenty of big ones. You don't reach the playoffs without winning the big ones.

They used to say the same thing about Miami and Don Shula and Dallas and Tom Landry, but not any more.

And they no longer can say that about Oakland and John Madden either.

X

Ted Marchibroda

In 1975 during his very first year as head coach of a floundering Baltimore Colt organization, Ted Marchibroda turned a team which had a 2-12 record the previous season into a Division champion with a 10-4 mark.

His performance as a rookie head coach earned him NFL Coach of the Year honors, and once again established Baltimore as a power in the Eastern Division of the AFC.

Many honors were justifiably bestowed upon Marchibroda after his great success during his first year with the Colts, but undoubtedly the greatest honor that any coach can receive was accorded him before the start of the 1976 season when his players backed him solidly against front office pressure being exerted against him.

Marchibroda justified the faith placed in him by directing the Colts into the playoffs for the second straight year.

As a college quarterback, Marchibroda enjoyed great success at both St. Bonaventure and the University of Detroit and was one of the nation's leading passers.

He was a first-round draft choice of the Pittsburgh Steelers in 1955, and after spending a year in the military service, he returned to the Steelers to become the second leading passer in the NFL in 1956.

He began his coaching career as offensive backfield coach for the Washington Redskins in 1961 under Bill McPeak. In 1966, he joined George Allen's staff at Los Angeles and when Allen was named head coach of the Redskins, Ted came along with George and was his offensive coordinator until he was selected as the Baltimore coach.

Marchibroda was born in Franklin, Pa., on March 15, 1931.

Baltimore 10, Miami 7

(Overtime)

1975 NFL GAME

By Ted Marchibroda

My greatest game as a head coach in the National Football League was played on December 15, 1975, in Baltimore during my first season with the Colts.

It was a 10-7 victory over the Miami Dolphins in an overtime game, and to many Baltimore fans, the game rates on a par with the famous 1958 Colt championship win over the New York Giants in another contest that was decided during an extra period.

In some ways, beating Miami could be considered a feat even greater than the 1958 victory since, unlike the veteran '58 Colts, we were a young team facing a well-seasoned club, and the pressure of going into a sudden death situation which would decide the Eastern Division title was tremendous.

There is nothing like experience when playing under extra pressure, and Miami had the edge in that department. Not only had many of their players been in overtime games before, but they had been Super Bowl champions in 1972 and 1973.

We had about 20 players who were either rookies or second year men. In all, I would say that about 90 percent of our squad had never before been involved in a game of this importance.

For all intents and purposes, our game against Miami was a championship one. After a slow start that found us losing four of our first five games, we had won our next seven in a row and were in second place in our Division with an 8 and 4 record.

In the five years that Don Shula had coached Miami, they had never missed the playoffs, and as Division leader with a 9 and 3 record, a win or a tie against us would make it six in a row for them.

We were determined to keep our playoff hopes alive after we had made such an impressive comeback. We had lost to Oakland, Los Angeles, Buffalo, and New England on successive weeks early in the season, and each of these games had been close enough so that we could have won any of them.

We were really disappointed when we lost to New England, 21-10. Losing to the Raiders, Rams, and Bills had been bad enough, but they were really tough teams. The Patriots were no slouches, but we felt we could beat them. When we didn't, I felt as though we hit bottom.

Sometimes when you reach a point like that, the losers stay there while the winners snap out of it and bounce back. Thank goodness, we were able to put it all together after our loss to New England.

During our string of seven straight wins, we had beaten Miami, 33-17, in the Orange Bowl so we knew we were capable of defeating them again. However, we also realized that any time you are up against a Don Shula-coached team you are in for a tough afternoon.

We hoped to jump off to an early lead. Bob Griese was hurt, and with Don Strock starting in his place, we wanted to put as much pressure as possible on Don. This could be accomplished by forcing Miami to play catch-up football and throw the ball more than they wanted to. Since Strock had not played much all season, we figured that he would have difficulty passing against us, and we wanted to keep him under pressure.

If we could contain them on first-down plays and get Strock passing on long-yardage downs, we would be in a good position to win.

We didn't plan to blitz any more than we might normally do in a game. Our defensive unit, although lacking the experience

Miami had, consistently came up with the big play so I felt no need to do anything different in this game.

Offensively, we wanted to have an even balance between our running and passing. That's always the ideal situation against a team of Miami's calibre, but it was Bert Jones' game to call, and once our offense is on the field, the play-calling is all his responsibility.

I had reached that decision with him during the Spring when we met and talked football for weeks. I told him then that I did not want him to be another Sonny Jurgenson, Roman Gabriel, Billy Kilmer or any other great quarterback. I wanted him to be himself . . . to play his own game . . . to assume responsibilities . . . to be a leader.

Since Bert is a great football talent with a character that equals his talent, I was certain that he would be more effective if he had full responsibility, and his record certainly speaks for itself.

Bert enjoys playing pro football as much as he enjoyed playing in high school and college, and that's the secret to playing winning football. The monetary rewards are important, but the love of the game must come first. You must play with the same intensity, the same desire in pro football as you did when you were playing without any pay. Bert's that way and so are many of the players on our squad.

We had an excellent week of practice before the Miami game. It was a normal week in every way except that I could feel tenseness building all week. At a meeting the night before the game, I told the players that it was only natural that they should feel uptight before a game like this, but it would go away once the referee blew the whistle for the opening kickoff.

I hoped that I had been able to help them be a bit more relaxed and asked if anyone had anything he would like to say. Joe Ehrmann got up and stammered—obviously joking—"N-n-no, n-not I." The players broke up.

Then, when I started to talk to the team again, I started to stutter, but in my case, it was not intended. The team howled, and it all helped break the tension.

In the locker room before the game, it was a little quieter than usual, but you could feel electricity in the air. It was a championship game for us, and everyone knew it.

While the players were getting dressed, I moved around the room, talking to individual players about their assignments and reviewing general offensive plans with our quarterbacks.

We had won the toss and elected to receive, and Bruce Laird came through with a beautiful run of 53 yards to the Miami 42. I could not have been more pleased since this put us in great position to score first and put the pressure on Strock as we had planned.

Our offensive unit rushed out on the field, but it wasn't to the Miami 42. We had been caught clipping on the play, and instead of having excellent field position, we had our backs to the wall on our own 11-yard line.

Three conservative running plays netted us only six yards, and we had to give up the ball. Miami took over on our 47, and early in the game, they now had the good field position that we had wanted. A short pass and two runs gave them a first down on our 36, and then Strock attempted to surprise us by going for the bomb against our cornerback Lloyd Mumphord to Howard Twilley in the end zone.

This had been a year when opposing teams tried time and again to go after Mumphord with the long pass, but just as he had done all season, Lloyd rarely was beaten. He stayed with Twilley all the way and made a fine interception in the end zone to stop the Miami threat.

I hoped that this would give us a shot in the arm, and with Jones mixing his running and passing plays effectively, we moved to the Miami 36 where we faced a fourth and one.

In our first game against Miami, when we had a fourth and one situation, we gambled and lost. Recalling that we had failed the last time, I gave some thought to trying to kick the ball out of bounds and put Miami in bad field position, but I finally decided to let our team go for the first down.

This decision was based on a number of reasons. First of all, it was early in the game. Secondly, we had been moving the ball very well on this drive, going from our own 20-yard line 44 yards on nine plays. We had the momentum, and I definitely felt that we could make it. Actually, it was more of a gut feeling.

Part of the decision to go for it was based on the fact that it isn't that simple to have your punter kick out-of-bounds inside the 10. You are putting tremendous pressure on your kicker, and many times he will just kick the ball into the end zone. If that were the case in this situation, we would have gained only 16 yards and would have lost the chance to keep our drive going. Making a first down on a play like this is certain to give your team a lift. It was a worthwhile gamble, but we lost when Bill Olds tried the left side and was held without any gain.

As it turned out, the gamble did not hurt us since Miami was forced to kick the ball back to us.

The first quarter ended scoreless with each team being able to make only two first downs. We had started all four of our drives that period from poor field positions—once from the 11, once from the 14, once from the 20, and finally from the 21. In contrast, Miami had much better field position, but our defense was doing its job.

Starting on our 21-yard line on the final play of the first quarter, we rolled up four first downs in a row and had a first down on the Miami 14 with a great chance to get on the board first.

Lydell Mitchell gained a yard around left end, and Jones, back to pass on second down, could find no one open and ran for another yard. Jones passed over the middle to Roger Carr, but Barry Hill broke up the play, saving a touchdown. On fourth and eighth from the 12, Toni Linhart tried a 29-yard field goal, but he was wide to the right.

Helped by a 24-yard pass play, Miami had a first down on

our 30 as time was running out for the half, but we forced them to go for a 45-yard field goal, and Garo Yepremian's attempt was wide to the left.

We had the ball on our 28 with 56 seconds left, and with all three time-outs remaining for Miami, it wasn't very likely that we could run the clock out solely with our running game, which had not been very effective the first half. Bert tried a bomb to Glenn Doughty down the left sideline, but it was overthrown. Bert was sacked by linebacker Bob Matheson for a 12-yard loss, and a screen pass to Don McCauley picked up 11 but left us in a punting situation with fourth and 11 on our 27.

Only ten seconds remained, and a good kick could end the half, but defensive end Vern DenHerder busted through to block the kick. While the ball was bouncing around, Stan White was charged with punching the ball to our 43, and we were penalized back to our 18.

With three seconds remaining on the clock, we had given Miami another chance to get on the board with a field goal, and although I wasn't too worried when Yepremian had tried one from his 45, I knew that he was far more consistent from 35 yards out.

Giving them three points with just seconds left wasn't the best way for us to leave the field at half time, but luckily Yepremian was wide to his left again.

Little did we realize at the time how important the two missed field goals by Miami and the one missed by us would be.

I don't think that anyone had believed that two high scoring teams like Miami and Baltimore could go through an entire half without either scoring, but despite the fact that no one scored, it had been an interesting and well played first half.

Even though we never started from good field position, we moved the ball fairly well. But to move 80 yards or more on any drive against a Miami defense was just too tough a job.

If you go by statistics, we outplayed Miami. We had nine first downs to their five, out-rushed them 72 to 68, and out-passed them 76 to 36. We ran 40 offensive plays to their 22. Jones was nine for 15 in passing, and Strock was three for eight with one interception. We were five for 11 on third down conversions, and Miami was one for five.

I was satisfied with our performance and told the team that we were right where we wanted to be. We reviewed our assignments and went over the blocked kick to make sure that wouldn't happen again.

I was especially pleased with the type of game Jones was calling. Before the season had started, I told our coaching staff that in order for us to be successful, Jones would have to mature into a 30-year-old quarterback at age 25. Bert did just that in the first half against Miami.

Bert's nature is to go for the big play, but fully aware that he could not afford to make any mistakes in this important game, he called a more conservative game than one would expect from him.

Although I am sure that he might have been tempted to go for the long pass more often, he concentrated on balancing his running game with short passes. Of the nine passes he completed in the first half, the longest was for 16 yards.

That first half performance by Bert convinced me that he had fully matured as a quarterback, and when we took the field for the second half, I was confident that we would win the game.

The third quarter was pretty much a defensive battle until Nat Moore ran back one of our punts 28 yards to our 27-yard line. On third and seven from our 24, Strock hit Larry Seiple, who made the first down by inches.

Norm Bulaich went off tackle for seven yards, and Mercury Morris went up the middle for five, and it was first and goal to go from the five.

When they got down there, I was hoping that they might fumble, but you have to face the inevitable. You know that a Shula-coached team is going to score from five yards out with four shots at the goal. You also know that you aren't going to shut out any of his teams for an entire game.

When Bulaich and Morris each made only a yard on the next

two plays, it looked like we might have a chance of getting away with only a field goal scored against us, but on third down, Morris went around left end for the first score of the game.

Once the play started, I could see that there was no way we were going to stop it. It was a combination of some great blocking and Mercury's speed. He just out-ran everyone to the corner of the end zone. He was so far ahead of his closest defender that he ran into the end zone with his hands extended over his head.

The third quarter ended with Miami leading, 7-0. They had completely dominated the period with five first downs to our one. They were four for six on third-down conversions, and we were 0 for three.

As the teams changed sides for the final period, Jones came over to the sidelines and asked me if he was doing the right thing. I told him that we were still in the ball game and to continue with our basic game plan.

The first time that we had possession of the ball in the fourth quarter it was on our own 14-yard line. Once again, we had to start from poor field position, but this time we had better success.

On a 13-play drive, Bert called six running plays and seven pass plays, hitting on six of the passes. The longest of any of these passes was for 11 yards. Bert, once again, was proving his maturity, giving up his favorite long pass for the shorter passes that were working so well.

One of the key plays in this drive came on a third and ten from our own 49. Bert passed over the middle to Mitchell, just short of the first down, but Lydell broke two tackles to get this crucial first down which kept our drive alive.

Then on second and six from Miami's 34, Bert was under tremendous pressure on a blitz and barely got the ball off to Mitchell, who again broke a tackle to pick up an 11-yard gain.

A Jones pass to Ray Chester gave us another first down on the 11, and Mitchell ran off the left side for five yards. Lydell then ran around left end to put us on the board at 9:30 of the final period.

On the try for the extra point which we needed to tie the

game, the snap was quite high, but Marty Domres pulled the ball down and had it placed in the proper spot to make it a routine kick for Linhart. Domres' alert play showed the importance of having an experienced holder for extra points and field goals.

On the next series, Morris fumbled after a five-yard gain, and Fred Cook recovered for us on our own 46. We felt that this was the big break that we had been waiting for, and since they had been moving the ball so well, we felt especially good about the recovery.

With less than four minutes to play at that time and with good field position to start a drive for the first time, we were determined to move into scoring position, but we never got close. Three penalties were called against us on the next four plays and we were backed up in our own territory with a fourth and 28 on our own 28-yard line.

Lee, with a career average of better than 41 yards per punt, hit one for only 33 yards to Nat Moore, who made a fair catch on his own 38.

Now, with only 2:36 left in the game, we had to keep Miami out of field goal range. Even though Yepremian had missed two tries in the first half, his record for the season was exceptionally good, and he was always a threat to hit a long one.

Three running plays gave them a first down on our 42, but then on a third and ten play, we got another break. Strock completed a 12-yard pass to Freddie Solomon, but Jim Langer was guilty of a personal foul. Instead of having a first down on our 30, it was now third and 25 on their own 44. Mike Barnes sacked Strock for an 11-yard loss, and Seiple was forced to punt from his own 33.

We were hoping for a blocked punt at this stage, but Seiple got off a 42-yard kick to Howard Stevens. Stevens caught the ball on his own 25, dodged one tackler and then, behind some beautiful blocking, ran 27 yards to Miami's 48.

Only 18 seconds remained, but with a quarterback like Bert Jones, it was enough time to get off one or two passes which could get us close enough for a shot at a field goal.

Bert's first pass to Doughty down the middle was well thrown, but Glenn was hit hard as he was going up for the ball, and the pass was incomplete. Throwing under great pressure, another pass from Bert to Doughty was too high, and then as time ran out, Bert failed on a desperation pass into the end zone.

We lost the toss of the coin, and that can be disastrous in an overtime game since the opponent can score before you ever get your hands on the ball.

However, I told our team that if we continued to play the same type of ball that we had up until then, we could beat them.

Hubie Ginn took the kickoff on his seven and almost broke loose as he returned the ball 30 yards to his 37. Morris gave them a first down on their 49 on two running plays, and it was crisis time again. A running play sandwiched between two incomplete passes forced Seiple to punt from our 47, and we were anxiously awaiting our first chance to do something in the extra period.

I watched Seiple as he put his foot to the ball, and then as I followed the ball all the way, my heart began to sink as I saw the ball go out of bounds. I could not tell exactly where the ball had gone out, but I knew it was inside the ten. When they marked it on the four, I was most disheartened. Our backs were against the wall; we were 96 yards away from the Miami goal line.

I gave Bert no special instructions as he left my side. I had given him the responsibility of calling the plays, and I wasn't about to take it away from him now. I could not have been more pleased with the first play he called. It was the one that I would have called. It was a play we call 25 Hunch, and it's our most basic play. Mitchell took the ball up the middle for a six yard gain, and this call by Bert set the tempo for the remainder of the drive.

McCauley went off right guard for four yards, and on third and one, on a play designed strictly for short yardage, Bill Olds powered his way for 11 yards and a first down on the 24.

Jones now had some breathing room, but trying to pass on the next play, he could find no one open and was forced to take a ten-yard loss. Once again, Bert showed his maturity by taking the loss instead of gambling by throwing the ball up for grabs.

Bert passed to McCauley for five yards, setting up a third and 15 situation on our own 19. Long yardage, deep in your own territory, Miami knew we had to complete a pass or give up the ball, and pass Jones did. He called a play identical to the one in the fourth period when we needed 10 yards. Now, we needed 15 yards, but it wasn't necessary for Bert to tell the receivers they had to run a longer pattern.

Bert had the option of going to Mitchell or Chester on this play. Chester ran a great pattern and really extended his entire body to make a leaping catch on the 34 before falling out-of-bounds on the 36. This was without doubt the most important play of the entire game.

Jones continued to mix his running and passing plays well, but when he reached the Miami 44, Bert Jones, the great passer, the quarterback who really loves to put the ball in the air, did not call a single pass play the rest of the game. He ground out the yardage in small chunks on seven consecutive running plays, and on fourth and three from the 14, Linhart kicked a 31-yard field goal with just 2:16 left in the overtime.

It was a great finish to a great game. It certainly was my greatest game as head coach of the Colts.

The drive that had started on the four-yard line and wound up with the winning field goal was the greatest drive that I have ever seen as a player, coach or spectator.

What made it so great was the fact that we were under a tremendous amount of pressure. We needed to get points. If we failed, a tie would have put us out of contention.

When I think back about that 10-7 victory, I like to say that our team played Colt football that afternoon. By that, I mean that every player gave of himself as much as he was capable of giving.

That's the attitude and type of performance which will enable the Colts to continue playing winning football.

XI

Don McCafferty

Don McCafferty spent a long apprenticeship as an assistant coach, and in 1970, when a head coaching position finally beckoned, the six-foot, five-inch former Ohio State tackle was ready for the challenge.

In his very first season as top man with the Baltimore Colts, he guided the team to pro football's world championship by defeating Dallas on a field goal in the closing seconds of Super Bowl V.

Don had spent ten years as an assistant at Kent State University and 11 years as an aide to Weeb Ewbank and Don Shula at Baltimore before the No. 1 spot became his.

After graduating from Ohio State, McCafferty was signed by the New York Giants, who shifted him to end during the 1946 season. He was released by the Giants before the start of the 1947 season and landed with their farm team in Jersey City.

He tried his hand as a high school teacher in Cleveland before receiving an offer from Kent State to coach.

In 1956, when Ewbank offered him a job with Baltimore, Don turned it down, preferring the security at Kent State, but two years later, Ewbank again invited Don to join his staff and this time he accepted. He served as end coach under Ewbank and offensive coordinator Shula.

As head coach of the Colts, McCafferty balked at front office interference with his coaching operation and was released after five games of the 1972 season.

Don became head coach of the Detroit Lions in 1973, but his very promising career came to a tragic end before the start of the 1974 season when he died from a heart attack.

Baltimore 21, Chicago 20
1970 NFL GAME

By Don McCafferty

We won the world's professional football championship the very first year that I was head coach so it would almost seem natural to select the win over Dallas in the Super Bowl as my most memorable game.

I did give considerable thought to Super Bowl V, since it was a fantastic game and a great victory for us, but in the long run, I felt that Baltimore's 21-20 triumph over the Chicago Bears on November 29, 1970, in Baltimore, is the game that stands foremost in my memories.

If we had not won that game, we probably would never have been in the Super Bowl in the first place.

Two weeks before the game with the Bears, we wound up in a tie with Buffalo when we should have beaten them, and just one week later, we had lost 34-17 to the Miami Dolphins, a team we had clobbered, 35-0, in our first meeting.

It seemed like we were going downhill, and we realized that a loss to Chicago could mean the last straw for us.

Doomsday appeared to be setting in as we trailed the Bears, 17-0, after only seven minutes in the first quarter, but instead of completely collapsing, our ball club fought back with all the courage you would expect from a team of championship calibre.

This was a tough Chicago Bears team we were playing, even though their win-loss record wasn't very impressive. The Bears are always tough and seem to give Baltimore a great deal of trouble every time we play them.

They may not beat you as far as the score is concerned, but they whip you physically and soften you up for your next opponent. I'm always happy when a game against the Bears is over and our casualty list isn't too bad.

When I first met with our squad on the Tuesday before the Chicago game, I chewed them out for the sloppy way they had played against Miami. That has always been one of the most distasteful things for me to do as a coach. I wish that it could be avoided, but you can't mince words with your players. If they make mistakes, if they loaf or shirk their duties, you have to tell it to them the way it is.

You don't have to holler and scream at the players. I learned that was unnecessary during the years I played under Paul Brown at Ohio State. You can be just as effective in getting across your message without raising your voice.

The game against Miami had been a comedy of errors. We had dropped pass after pass. We fumbled a punt. We had allowed them to score much too easily on long plays, so I felt it necessary to let them know just how poorly they had performed.

The lecture didn't last long, and I told them to forget about last week and start preparing for the Bears game.

Actually, our coaching staff had started preparation for the Bears on Monday. While the players had the day off to rest up, I met with the coaches to review the films of the Miami game. All coaches made notations about the performances of the players.

Then, we took a look at the films we had received of the Bears' games. We were worried about Chicago's defense. When you play against a team with a linebacker as great as Dick Butkus, you have your work cut out for you. Butkus was the key to the Bears' defense, and you have to plan on keeping your offensive plays as far away from him as possible.

On Tuesday, after our squad meeting, everyone took a look at the films of the Miami game. Then, the players broke into groups, and the coaches made constructive criticisms of the players' performances. This was followed by a short workout, mainly to get the players loosened up.

152

After a brief rest, the squad watched films of the Bears' games, and we checked our scouting reports about them. The day ended for the players with a discussion of our offensive and defensive plans for the game.

However, the day's work was not over for the coaches. We continued to work on our plans until 9:30 p.m. when we finally broke for dinner.

Wednesday was our offensive day. Both morning and afternoon sessions were devoted to testing our running and passing plays against the Chicago defense and trying to find the most effective.

The Bears had altered their defense in 1970 and were using a wide variety of defenses, including some unusual fronts, so we were experimenting against the different type coverage they had been using.

Thursday was our defensive day, and we had decided to make several changes in our starting lineup after reviewing the films of the Miami game. We moved Jimmy Duncan to right cornerback, put Ray May at left linebacker, and decided to give Roy Hilton another shot at right end.

We spent that day concentrating on Chicago's short yardage running plays, and we were satisfied that we could contain their offense.

Friday was our combination day when we worked with both our offensive and defensive units. After a session of pass offense, pass defense, running offense, and defense against runs, we went into our two-minute drill which always seems to be the fun part of practice for the players.

Our week of practice ended on Saturday, which is our kicking day. We look at films showing both our and Chicago's kickoff returns, punts and field goal tries. Then, we go over exactly what we want to do on these plays.

The entire squad, along with the coaches, went to a motel in the evening, and after a snack at 9:30, the players were in their rooms for an 11 o'clock bed check.

The worst part of any week during the football season is the day of the game. It's rough on the players and coaches waiting around for the game to start. Of course, the players get taped and dressed and warm up for part of the time. But there always seems to be too much time to kill before the kickoff.

We reviewed some of the things we did during the past week, but there was no pep talk as such. We had been building up for all this week, and I thought we were ready for the Bears. Just before we took the field, Bob Vogel led the squad in prayer which is traditional before and after all our games.

We won the toss, and Jimmy Duncan ran the kickoff from the end zone back to our 28-yard line. Passes by John Unitas to Norm Bulaich and Eddie Hinton were dropped on the first two plays, and it looked like this was going to be Miami all over again. On third and ten, John passed again, and this time Ross Brupbacker, who was being used as a fourth linebacker by the Bears, intercepted on our 41-yard line and ran the ball back to the 36.

The Bears picked up 16 yards on two plays and had a first down on our 20. Jack Concannon passed to George Farmer, who made the catch at the goal line for the touchdown.

On that play, Duncan, our right cornerback, was late adjusting to an audible defensive call. He had been expecting some inside help, and when he didn't get it, Farmer was left open and made an easy reception.

Mac Percival booted the extra point and after only 2:11 of the first period, we were behind, 7-0, and in the unenviable position of having to play catch-up football so early in the game.

Starting from our own 20 after the kickoff, Jerry Hill gained five yards over right tackle but then dropped a pass from Unitas at the line of scrimmage. On third and five, Ed O'Bradovich deflected a Unitas pass intended for Hill on an outlet valve, and George Seals was in the right spot at the right time to pick it off on our 22. Actually, Seals was still on the line of scrimmage because our offensive linemen had kept him from making a good rush.

The Bears could gain only one yard on three plays and settled for a 28-yard field goal by Percival. It was now 10-0, and only 3:40 had been played in the game.

On the very first play after the next kickoff, Unitas attempted a pass to Tom Mitchell, but Dick Daniels, Chicago's right safety, intercepted at our 43 and raced back to the 27.

It was hard to believe. Unitas had attempted six passes. Three were dropped and three were intercepted. It looked like we were really falling apart.

Concannon's pass to Dick Gordon in the end zone was overthrown, but Jerry Logan, our left safety, was charged with pass interference, placing the ball on the one-yard line. Everything was going against us.

After a running play failed, Concannon tossed to tight end Rich Coady in the end zone for the touchdown. Percival converted, and it was 17-0 at exactly seven minutes of the first period.

I just could not believe that our team had slipped so badly. We had won seven out of our first eight games before being tied by Buffalo and beaten by Miami the last two weeks. The slump of the last two weeks was continuing, and our hopes for a championship were rapidly disappearing.

When you are coaching on the sidelines, you hear the crowd and the noises, but you rarely hear anything an individual in the stands says. This day, I heard only too clearly one fan yell: "Hey, McCafferty! What do you think of your defensive changes now?"

Well, our being behind, 17-0, had nothing to do with our defense. The offense had turned the ball over three times in our own territory, and we were lucky it wasn't 21-0.

It all happened so fast that I didn't even give any thought of taking Unitas out of there. Even if I had thought about it, I probably would have stayed with him. You know that a passer as great as Unitas is going to snap out of it sooner or later, and when you have to play catch-up football, I guess I'd rather go with John than anyone else.

We managed to get through the next series of plays without an interception, and when we kicked to the Bears' 27-yard line, it was the first time that they were starting from their own territory.

They didn't stay there very long as Don Shy broke over the middle, raced up the left side for a 45-yard gain before Charlie

Stukes, our left cornerback, tackled him on our 16 to prevent another touchdown.

Following an incompleted pass to Coady, Concannon tried to go to the air again, but Mike Curtis busted through to nail him for an eight-yard loss. Concannon passed to Farmer on the eight, but the Bears had an ineligible player downfield and were penalized back to the 39.

That penalty was the first favorable break we received, and relieved us of some of the pressure. The Bears tried to surprise us with a draw on third and 32, but we were ready and it was good for only a yard. Percival came in to attempt a field goal from the 45, but it was wide and we took over on our 20.

We seemed to come alive at this point. Unitas hit on three passes, and we had a first down on the Bears' 44 as the first period ended.

At long last, we were in Bear territory. A pass to Hinton was almost intercepted by Chicago's right cornerback Joe Taylor, but Unitas came right back on a screen pass to Mitchell, our tight end, who stayed in his block and then slipped out into the flat.

That gave us a first down on the 28, and Unitas called a beautiful trap pass play that worked to perfection and put the ball on the one. This play gave every indication of being a running play. Sam Havrilak, the running back, came out of the backfield and headed towards the linebacker as if to block him.

The guard pulled as he would on a running play, and when the linebacker decided to rush in, Havrilak moved out. Unitas was under a heavy rush but tossed the ball quickly to Sam, who almost made it all the way.

Hill hit left guard for the touchdown from the one, and Jim O'Brien's kick cut the Bears' lead to 17-7 at 57 seconds of the second period.

The game settled down to a defensive battle until late in the quarter when Ron Gardin, our rookie safety, returned a punt to the Bears' 45. A pass and then a running play gave us a first down on the 30. On third and eight from the 28, John hit Havrilak on a screen pass which was just good enough for a first down on the 20.

Hill tried the middle for no gain, and a pass to Hinton was incomplete. On third and ten, Unitas could not find anyone open downfield far enough for the first down, and he had to throw to Mitchell as an outlet. Mitchell could gain only seven yards, leaving us three yards short of a first down.

Unitas called time out and came to the sideline to discuss the situation with me. It was a major decision. There was only a minute left to play in the half. Do you go for the sure three points with a field goal or do you take the gamble and try for the touchdown? If you fail to get the touchdown, you're in serious trouble, but if you make the touchdown, you can leave the field trailing only 17-14 and with momentum to carry you through to victory in the second half.

I decided that, with a clutch quarterback like Unitas, the gamble would not be too great, so I told John to call for a 40 pass. On this play, we have two receivers, Hinton and Roy Jefferson, who are No. 1 targets, depending upon what the defense shows. Unitas passed to Hinton, who made a great one-handed grab just before stepping out-of-bounds on the seven-yard line for the first down.

It's funny what some people will read into a game. After it was all over, there was talk that Unitas decided to throw to Hinton because Eddie had previously dropped two passes, and it would help him regain his confidence.

Hell, we weren't interested in anything but getting the first down. When the two teams lined up, I knew that Unitas was going to throw to Hinton because the man on Jefferson was right up on him while the man on the left covering Hinton was off a bit.

On the next play, Unitas and Jefferson teamed up on another perfectly executed play for the touchdown. This was a quick take-off play which we normally use for a bomb, but in this case, Jefferson made a quick move and ran to the corner of the end zone while Unitas took a couple of steps back and laid the ball out there.

Naturally, we felt a bit happier being behind only 17-14 at the half after having fallen behind 17-0 in the first seven minutes.

Unitas was passing better after his horrible start, but our running game still was quite bad. We had been able to gain only 38 yards rushing on 14 carries. On the other hand, Unitas, after missing on his first six passes, was 14 out of 25 for 142 yards.

The Bears were using a three-man line with four linebackers, and it was confusing us. The extra linebacker was making the big difference as far as our running game was concerned, and when one of those linebackers is a fellow named Butkus, it has to hurt you.

We spent much of the half time reviewing those plays which had worked well and discussing others which we thought could be better exploited in the second half.

The third quarter turned into a punting duel with neither team being able to put a long drive together. Late in the period, Unitas had his fourth interception of the day, but at least this one was in Bear territory, and coupled with a clipping penalty, set them back to their 11.

Chicago moved to our 41 where on fourth and two, Percival came in for a 48-yard field goal try. Percival faked the kick and caught us by surprise by going downfield himself and catching a pass from Concannon. Duncan saved a touchdown by nailing Percival on the 23.

Our defensive backs had been completely fooled. Normally, on a long field goal attempt, they will watch the ends or the fullback in protecting against a fake, but in this case, it was the kicker who ran out for the pass, and nobody covered him.

Our defense held after that, and the Bears were forced to settle for a 27-yard field goal by Percival, giving them a 20-14 lead at 3:19 of the fourth period.

We were in trouble once again soon after the kickoff when Unitas had his fifth pass of the day intercepted. John was supposed to throw to Bulaich on a halfback option play, but Norm was covered and John whipped the ball to Tom Nowatzke, who was coming out of the backfield on the opposite side. Butkus, who was everywhere you looked that afternoon, leaped high and made a great one-handed interception on our 43.

Our defense took over and held the Bears to seven yards on three plays, and Percival missed a 43-yard field goal attempt.

The clock was becoming a factor. Getting close enough for a field goal wasn't good enough. We had to go all the way.

There were only about five minutes remaining when we took over on our own 24 after Gardin made a fair catch of a punt. Unitas passed 22 yards to John Mackey and then hit John on a 54-yard scoring play.

Mackey was a decoy on this play, with Jimmy Orr the primary target on an individual outside pattern. Unitas saw that they were using a zone on Orr and since the pattern he was running wasn't good against zone coverage, John looked for his secondary receiver, Jefferson, on the opposite side. But they had a zone there, too.

John glanced down the middle, and there was Mackey all by himself. Unitas ducked away from a Chicago lineman and zipped the ball to Mackey, who made an easy catch on the 30, put a move on Gary Lyle, the free safety, at the 14 and went into the end zone standing up.

Later on, we found out that the Bears had messed up their coverage on the play. An audible had been called to switch from the zone, but someone failed to hear the change, and Mackey was allowed to get free. It was a lucky break for us, but we deserved a good one after all the bad luck we'd had earlier in the game.

When O'Brien, our rookie place-kicker, booted the tie-breaking extra point, the clock showed 3:47 left to play—plenty of time for the Bears to get within field goal range.

Once again, our defense was great, holding the Bears and forcing them to kick from their 13.

Only two minutes remained, and I told Unitas to make sure he kept the ball on the ground. You usually don't have to worry about a quarterback like Unitas in a spot like that, but I kept remembering a similar situation earlier that year when we were leading Boston, 7-6, with about three minutes left in the game.

It was third and two from our own 45, and John decided to pass. The seconds that the ball was in the air seemed like hours, but when Jefferson made the catch and went 55 yards for a touchdown, it was the first chance I had to smile all day.

This time, Unitas wasn't about to give me any heart failure. He stayed on the ground and actually got us close enough for a shot at a field goal, but O'Brien's boot from the 44 rolled dead on the 10.

The Bears still had one more chance, but four plays gained only one yard, and victory was ours.

However, for a while it looked like we might have won the battle but lost the war. Our casualty list, always high after a Bears game, was worse than usual. Jim Bailey, our defensive tackle, was lost for the season. Fred Miller, our other defensive tackle, was injured, along with three offensive guards, Glenn Ressler, John Williams, and Cornelius Johnson; offensive tackle Bob Vogel; defensive end Bubba Smith, and halfback Norm Bulaich.

Not one player complained about the physical beating they had taken from the Bears. They were pleased—and justly so—about their courageous comeback which eventually carried Baltimore into the Super Bowl.

XII

Earle "Greasy" Neale

Earle (Greasy) Neale was enshrined in pro football's Hall of Fame in 1969, but some 60 years before that, back in Parkersburg, West Virginia, he was already destined for immortality.

Neale not only was captain of his high school football team but he served as its coach as well and led the team to a state championship.

His fame continued as a freshmen at West Virginia Wesleyan in 1912. Before Wesleyan's big game against its deadly rival, West Virginia, a team it had never beaten, Neale prevailed upon his coach to use a new play and then proceeded to lead his team to a 19-14 upset victory.

Neale coached at Marietta, West Virginia Wesleyan, Washington and Jefferson, Virginia, West Virginia, and Yale, but he is probably best remembered for his 1921 Washington and Jefferson team which went undefeated in ten games and then held heavily favored California to a scoreless tie in the Rose Bowl.

Greasy entered the pro coaching ranks in 1941 at Philadelphia, and three years later, he had the once-lowly Eagles in second place.

In 1947, the Eagles won the Eastern Division title only to lose the NFL title to the Chicago Cardinals, 28-21, but the next two years, Philadelphia reigned as the world's champions with a 7-0 win over the Cardinals in 1948 and a 14-0 victory over Los Angeles in 1949.

Those two championship Philadelphia teams are regarded by many as being among the all-time great teams to play in the NFL.

Neale was born November 5, 1891, in Parkersburg and died in West Palm Beach, Fla., November 3, 1973.

Philadelphia 28
Washington 24

1964 NFL GAME

By Earle (Greasy) Neale

It has been more than 20 years, but it is not difficult for me to remember my most memorable game as a pro coach. I had to look up some of the details, but I will never forget that day in Washington, D.C., when my Philadelphia Eagles were trailing Sammy Baugh and the Redskins, 24-0, in the third period, and we wound up winning, 28-24.

At that time, October 27, 1946, our victory was called the greatest comeback by any team in the history of the National Football League. I believe that game still stands today as the greatest comeback of all time.

We came to Washington with a 2-2 record, knowing that a defeat would just about eliminate us from the Eastern Division title. We had started the season in great fashion, beating Los Angeles and Boston, but the next two weeks were disastrous ones as we lost to Green Bay and the Chicago Bears.

The Redskins were leading the Eastern Division with an undefeated record of three wins and a tie, and they needed a win against us to stay ahead of the New York Giants.

We all knew that Redskin coach Turk Edwards would have his team up for this game, and we worked hard all week, setting up defenses against Baugh's passes and planning some new offensive plays.

It didn't help our game plan when we learned that Steve Van Buren would be out of the line-up with an injury. Your running game has to be affected when you lose a great running back like Van Buren.

However, we were encouraged when on the second play of the game, Ernie Steele cracked the Redskin line and went for 43 yards. He would have gone all the way, but Dick Todd saved the touchdown by tackling Steele on the Washington 27-yard line.

We couldn't move the ball after that, and the Redskins took over. We looked good in holding Washington on their first series of offensive plays, but when we got the ball again, we ran into trouble right away as Jack Jenkins intercepted a Tommy Thompson pass and ran 28 yards down the sidelines to the Eagle 18-yard line.

Washington moved on the ground to the two, from where Sal Rosato went over for the touchdown. Dick Poillon kicked the extra point, and Washington led, 7-0.

Not too much later in the first period, Wilbur Moore intercepted another Thompson pass on his own 40 and ran it back 30 yards to our 30-yard line. The Redskins could gain only one yard on three plays, and on fourth down, they were forced to settle for a field goal by Poillon from the 29. That made it 10-0, Washington, and the first period ended that way.

We didn't look any better in the second period, but we did manage to keep the Redskins from scoring until late in the quarter. Then, Thompson had his third pass intercepted, this time by Clyde Ehrhardt, who grabbed the ball on the Eagle 45 and ran it back all the way to the seven. Rosato took it over from there, and Poillon added the extra point, making it Washington 17, Philadelphia 0.

There was only a minute and a half left when the Redskins kicked off to us on the 14. On the very first play, Allie Sherman, who was then in at quarterback, tried to hand off the ball, but there were all kinds of confusion in our backfield. I don't even know who was supposed to get the ball. All I remember was the ball was suddenly rolling towards the end zone, and Ted Lapka fell on it under the goal post for another Redskin touchdown. After Poillon kicked the extra point, it was 20-0, Washington, and we were a pretty unhappy team as we left the field at half-time.

We were an unhappy lot but were far from discouraged. The three Washington touchdowns and field goal were all set up as the result of our mistakes, and not because the Redskins were so superior to our ball club.

We just couldn't get going in that first half. It seemed like everything we did went wrong. Working out of the T formation, we weren't able to run or pass. Our blocking was especially bad on our passes, and Thompson wasn't being given a chance. It was no wonder that he had three interceptions.

We weren't too much better during the early part of the third period as far as moving the ball was concerned. The Redskins backed us up to our own one-yard line midway in the period, and when Jim Youell returned our punt to our 25-yard line, it didn't look too encouraging for us.

But then we got our first break as Rudy Smeja recovered Poillon's fumble on the 30. We lost three yards on two plays from the T formation, so I signalled Thompson to go into a single-wing-back spread formation. This was the formation that the former Redskin coach Ray Flaherty had used so effectively.

I decided that we had to shift away from the T because all three quarterbacks I had been using—Thompson, Zimmerman, and Sherman—were under too much pressure from the Redskin line.

On third down and 13 yards to go, Thompson was now eight yards back with plenty of time to throw, and he hit Steele over the middle for 17 yards and a big first down.

On that particular play, Bosh Pritchard was supposed to go down five yards and then cut out, but he had kept right on going down the field. I told Thompson to run the same play again, but this time to tell Pritchard to go only five yards down.

Pritchard ran the pattern right, and Thompson hit him with an eight-yard pass. Bosh slipped a little after making the catch, and Moore, a great defensive back, rushed in to tackle him, but Pritchard sidestepped him and went all the way for our first touchdown. The play covered 56 yards. Augie Lio kicked the extra point, and we trailed 24-7, with about six minutes left to play in the third period.

About three minutes later, we had another chance when we recovered a Washington fumble on their 15. We went into the single-wing-back formation again. Thompson passed to Jack Ferrante for five, and an offside penalty against the Redskins put the ball on the five.

Steele hit the center of the line to the one-yard line. Mel Bleeker tried the same spot, but he was stopped cold. Thompson then pitched out to Steele, who raced around end for our second touchdown. Lio again kicked the extra point, and we now trailed, 24-14.

In the fourth quarter, Thompson completely confused the Washington defense by shifting back and forth from the T to the single wing almost every other play. Starting from our own 35-yard line, Thompson passed most of the way to get us our third touchdown.

He hit Dick Humbert for 11 and Gil Steinke for 31. Steinke almost went all the way on that play, but Youell stopped him with a great tackle on the Redskin 19.

Thompson passed to Jim Castiglia for seven, and Steinke hit the middle for four and a first down on the eight-yard line. From the single wing, Thompson passed to Steinke on the five, and Gil broke away from a Redskin tackler to go across for the touchdown. Lio's extra point brought the score to 24-21 with just a little more than five minutes left.

We kicked off to the Redskins, hopeful of stopping them and getting another chance to score. With just under three minutes to play in the game, the Redskins had the ball on their own 40, with a fourth down coming up and one yard to go.

Baugh faced the decision of either punting and giving us another chance or going for the first down and then running out the clock. This is one of those calls that gives the Monday morning quarterbacks something to talk about the rest of the season.

Baugh apparently had confidence in Sal Rosato, who had shown good power in scoring two touchdowns in the first half, so he decided to go for the first down. But Ben Kish and Dick Humbert were right there when Rosato hit the line, and they stopped him cold.

We called a time out and Thompson came over to the sideline to talk with me. I told him to try 71 down and out to the sideline in order to bring in the Redskins' defensive back who was covering Ferrante, and to then try 71 long. On 71 down and out Thompson overshot Ferrante, but on 71 long, the defensive back whose name I don't recall, ran in to cover Ferrante again. This time, instead of cutting out, Ferrante just kept right on going down the field and when he turned at the goal line, he was all alone.

That was really a beautiful sight to see Ferrante standing there all by himself, and Thompson hit him with a perfect strike to put us ahead. Lio again kicked the extra point, making it 28-24.

There were now only about 90 seconds left in the game, but when a great passer like Sammy Baugh is in there against you, anything can happen.

We kicked off short to the 35-yard line so that none of the Washington fast deep men could get a chance for a long run back. Baugh went into the single-wing-back formation they had discarded three years before, and we had stolen from them. He picked up two first downs, and then on a long pass which could have won the game for them, Ernie Steele intercepted and that was the ball game.

And what a ball game to win! Nothing at all worked from the T formation for more than half the game, but once we shifted to the single wing and kept mixing it with the T, we were able to work our plays well.

This was really a team effort. It has to be when you are 24 points behind in the third quarter and you are able to beat a great quarterback like Sammy Baugh.

And without meaning to slight any of my other players, I can't help but say something about the play of Tommy Thompson. After having three of his passes intercepted and turned into scores in the first half, he performed magnificently from both the single wing and the T in the second half and wound up completing 18 out of 24 passes.

That was a memorable performance in my most memorable game as a pro coach.

XIII

Don Shula

Don Shula never had a losing season during his seven years as head coach of the Baltimore Colts, but when he took over the reins of the Miami Dolphins in 1970, his record was in jeopardy with an expansion team that had never enjoyed a winning season.

Shula not only had another winning season in his very first year in Miami, but he had a remarkable season, with a 10-4 record to gain the American Conference playoffs.

That was only the beginning for Shula. In 1972, he led Miami to a perfect record with 17 straight wins, including the Super Bowl, and followed this with a second straight Super Bowl win in 1973.

Miami was Eastern Division champs in 1974 but lost in the playoffs, and in 1975, Miami missed the playoffs for the first time in six years despite a 10-4 record.

In 1976, injuries to key players resulted in a 6-8 record, Shula's first losing season as a head coach. But in spite of all the problems Shula faced in '76, four of those games were lost by a total of only 11 points.

With a grand total of 151 victories in 14 seasons, Shula is the most-winning active coach in the game today. He was the youngest coach ever to win over 100 games, and the first coach to take a team to the Super Bowl three years in a row.

Shula was a halfback at John Carroll College and a defensive

169

back for seven years with Cleveland, Baltimore, and Washington before serving as an assistant coach at the Universities of Virginia and Kentucky.

In 1960, he became a defensive coach for the Detroit Lions, and then assumed his first head coaching job with the Colts in 1963.

In his second year, the Colts won the Western Division title with a 12-2 record which included 11 straight wins. Shula was named Coach of the Year, an honor he would receive time and again.

Shula was born January 4, 1930 in Painesville, Ohio.

Baltimore 20, Los Angeles 14
1965 NFL GAME

by Don Shula

Climaxing the 1972 undefeated season with a Super Bowl victory over the Washington Redskins and then successfully defending our world's championship against Minnesota resulted in games which were most rewarding to me in many ways, but if I must select one game as my greatest, it would have to be the Baltimore-Los Angeles contest, played December 19, 1965, during my third season as head coach of the Colts.

The week leading up to this second meeting of the year against the Rams was the strangest and most unforgettable time that I have spent in my coaching career.

Injuries to our No. 1 quarterback and his understudy on successive Sundays created an almost unbelievable situation for me.

First, John Unitas, our great quarterback, was hurt during the Chicago Bears game. He suffered the worst type of knee injury when he was hit high and low from both sides. Our doctor gave me the unhappy news. Unitas needed immediate surgery and was out for the season.

There was still hope for us since Gary Cuozzo had done an excellent job for us earlier in the year when he was called upon to fill in for Unitas. Gary had proved his capability by throwing five touchdown passes to help us win and keep our momentum going.

The next week against Green Bay, lightning struck again. Cuozzo was carried off the field, and I can remember how depressed I was. His injury was diagnosed as a shoulder separation which required surgery that same evening.

It was hard to believe. Two weeks and two quarterbacks lost for the season. And if this wasn't enough of a handicap before a crucial game, we had one day less to prepare for the Rams since the game was scheduled for a Saturday. My only consolation was that things couldn't get any worse.

Following Cuozzo's operation, I met with my assistant coaches in an attempt to formulate some type of game plan to present to our football team at the Tuesday morning meeting.

Here we were, going into our 14th and final game of our regular season, needing a victory to stay alive in the tough Western Division. A win for Green Bay in its last game would sew up the title, but if the Packers lost, a win for us would give us the right to play the Eastern Division winners for the NFL championship. If Green Bay were held to a tie, it would mean a deadlock for first place and a special playoff game between us.

With so much riding for us on this final game, it was extremely difficult for members of our staff to mask their disappointment.

Don McCafferty, John Sandusky, and Dick Bielski, our offensive coaches, wondered how they could plan an offense without a quarterback. Charley Winner and Bill Arnspager, who handled our defensive units, realized how much more would be asked of them that week.

We were un unhappy group, but we weren't going to give up without a battle. Experience had taught us a long time ago that anything could happen in sports.

My first job, of course, was to select the player to be moved into the quarterback slot. There were only two men on the squad with quarterback experience in college, and neither had been used at that position during the four or five years they had played pro ball. One was Tom Matte of Ohio State, and the other was Bobby Boyd of Oklahoma. Both their colleges had featured the running game over the pass, and whatever passing they had done was on roll-outs as opposed to the drop-back technique used by Unitas and Cuozzo.

172

Having worked as a running back with us, Matte was the logical choice because of his superior knowledge of our offense. I called Matte Monday evening and told him he was the man, and in typical Matte fashion he assured me he'd give it his best. At that time I wasn't aware of how good the best of Tom Matte would be.

An old friend from Pittsburgh, Art Rooney, knowing of our problem, called to let me know that Ed Brown, a veteran quarterback, was available if something could be worked out to clear him through waivers. I wanted Ed even though his value would depend on how quickly he could get with us and how much of our system he could absorb in so short a time.

On Tuesday morning I met with our squad for the first time since we lost to Green Bay, and you couldn't imagine how low their spirits were. Somehow I had to make these players realize all wasn't lost and we still had a chance to win.

The plan I presented to them that day was a simple one: play defense. Don't make any offensive errors. Work for field position and make the kicking game win for us. All I got from the players was a lot of blank stares.

It got worse when we left the meeting room and started our light Tuesday morning workout. Matte called the first play in the huddle and took his team to the line of scrimmage. To my astonishment our defensive linemen rose in unison and began to laugh. They couldn't believe Matte's high-pitched voice. It definitely lacked the command of a John Unitas.

That afternoon I received a phone call from Woody Hayes, Matte's coach at Ohio State. Woody said he had read that Tom was to be my quarterback, and he wanted to call and assure me that I didn't have anything to worry about. I told Woody I appreciated his call, but down deep I was still very concerned.

Woody said Matte would make the big play in the toughest circumstances. He ended the conversation by saying Matte's only fault as a T-formation quarterback was his inability to get the snap from the center.

So there was nothing for me to worry about—nothing except a T-quarterback who couldn't execute the simplest but most important technique.

Now I was more anxious than ever to get Ed Brown, but later that afternoon the news from Pittsburg was far from encouraging. Acquiring Brown on waivers was not going to be as easy as anticipated.

Another club which obviously knew we were trying to get him stepped in and also claimed him, and this would mean either Pittsburgh or the Colts would have to ask the claiming club to withdraw so we could get him. I was hopeful this could be worked out but unhappy about the delay because time was more critical than ever.

Since we weren't sure of Brown, our offensive plans would have to be styled for Matte, definitiely not the "pocket" type ouarterback that a Brown would be.

A: we began our pre-game strategy, all our regular pro attack went out the window.

Normally, in preparing our game plan, we first decide on the number of offensive formations from which we want to run and pass. Sometimes we might feel that 10 to 12 sets of formations are needed in order to confuse the defense, and this requires a great deal of advance work, plus a seasoned quarterback.

Since we had neither the time nor the experienced quarterback, it was necessary to settle on a few things and attempt to do them well. Too many plays would only confuse Matte.

We decided three sets would be enough to stay simple and still give the defense enough to worry about.

We selected four basic running plays, two pass plays, plus a screen and a draw to work off each of these formations. Hopefully, this limited offense would give us some punch without putting too much pressure on Matte.

In addition to these plays, we thought Matte's running ability could be put to good use if he faked hand-offs on basic running plays and kept the ball himself. As it turned out, these "quarterback keep it" plays proved most effective.

Our practices that week resembled a high school team in its first week of fall football. Matte with the high-pitched voice, mass confusion in the huddle, uncertainty at the line of scrimmage, and finally the fumbles on the exchange from center that would stop any play before it started, did little to build my hopes.

Through it all, Matte kept his "cool." Tom had a medical history of a severe ulcer that at various times threatened to end his football career. He was constantly on medication, and if there was ever a time for it to act up, he now had a good excuse.

Looking back, I am continually amazed as to how he reacted to this intense pressure. Instead of his being the worry or "ulcer guy," he was the one who attempted to calm others. His attitude was: "Go out and give it your best shot." It was an approach which managed to give all of us confidence that somehow, some way, the best shot would be good enough.

Finally, some of the pieces began to fall in place. At times we actually resembled an offensive unit. Our four plays were being well executed, and the new quarterback-keep plays looked like they might take the Rams by surprise. There were even times when Matte managed to give a deeper pitch to his voice, and this gave us more confidence.

Before leaving for Los Angeles on Wednesday, we learned that Ed Brown had cleared waivers and would join us in California the next day. That would give him only two days to work out with us, but it was worth the effort. At this point, we would have been willing to try anything.

The minute Brown checked into our hotel, he was rushed to my suite along with Dick Szymanski, our center, and a couple of assistant coaches.

We gave Ed a list of plays that was even shorter and less confusing than the ones Matte had received. Instead of making Ed learn our numerical play calling system, each play was given a name. For example, 38 was our sweep to the right and 39 was our sweep left, but Ed would simply have to call "sweep right" or "sweep left," with no numbers involved.

His other running plays were: Trap, right or left; Short Trap, right or left; Dive, right or left; Fullback Slant, right or left; Fullback Draw, right or left; and Fullback or Halfback Screen, right or left.

175

His pass plays were limited to just two patterns. On one, he had the option of hitting the flanker on individual pattern, or the tight end on a zone pass. The second was a flood pattern to the weak side, with the flanker running an individual pattern in the event of single coverage or a "red-dog" by the defense.

He had only two formations to remember: flank and flank split.

That afternoon, Ed worked out with the team for the first time, and the "dry run" in the hotel room helped him in this first practice session. His experience was evident, and he quickly won the respect of our players.

I later learned the Rams had a "spy" watching us practice, and the fact Brown showed up kept them from concentrating too much on Matte and the type of offense he was running.

Friday, the day before the game, was devoted mostly to our kicking game, but because of our offensive predicament, we gave our "Matte offense" and our "Brown offense" one last review. The players were loose, and we all knew our title hopes were still alive.

The night before the game, our club owner, Carroll Rosenbloom, treated the squad to a dinner at one of Los Angeles' finest restaurants. The team spirit was high.

One of our players, however, missed the dinner because of a temperature and signs of the flu bug. No great concern. It was only Tom Matte.

Saturday morning at the pre-game meal Tom looked slightly under the weather but said he was ready to go. I reviewed with our quarterbacks the game plan and also the first series of plays I wanted to use.

These plays were singled out for a special purpose. We wanted to see the coverage the Rams were going to give us.

I planned to start Matte but use Brown on the second play. This was being done in order to determine at the outset if Los Angeles had planned different defensive tactics for our two new quarterbacks.

Our pre-game practice that day in the Coliseum was without a doubt the flattest and most unmoving that I have ever been associated with either as a coach or as a player. There wasn't any chatter and, more important, there was no execution. Matte, in warm up, didn't complete a pass, and Brown wasn't much better.

The pre-game practice is generally a good indication as to what to expect when the game starts, but in this instance I couldn't have been more wrong.

When we assembled in the dressing room for our last meeting before kickoff, I told the players I had never seen a worse pre-game practice, and unless our attitude changed, there would be no telling what the score might be against us.

After Don Shinnick led us in the "Lord's Prayer," a ritual with our team, I reviewed the first series of plays with the entire squad.

Then I said a final few words in an attempt to bring the players to the positive mental outlook so necessary before taking the field.

I told them that this was the most unusual game I had ever prepared for as a coach. Many strange things had happened to us, and we were now left with our backs against the wall. Our team could go one of two ways.

We could go through the motions of playing, end the season, and not be criticized too severely because the loss of Unitas and Cuozzo gave us a built-in excuse. The other alternative was to go out and overcome all obstacles . . . refuse to be outplayed . . . hustle and hit like never before . . . and be a winner.

I reminded them that the real test of each player is what he does under adverse conditions. I urged them to reach down for that something extra to help make the big play.

It would have to be up to the defense to win the game. Our offense must not make any big errors. We would have to work for field position and rely upon our kicking game to score for us.

I finished by telling them that not many teams at this stage still had a chance to win it all, and anything could happen out there. There was no reason why they could not accomplish this upset. I told them that above all they were to enjoy every minute of the game and go home proud of the way they had played.

As we left the dressing room for the kickoff, I could feel that the team was ready to give it a great effort.

Early in the game, I was proud of the job our defense was doing on quarterback Roman Gabriel and the Rams. This was a must. Without a great defense to keep the Rams from scoring, we would face the task of trying to come from behind with an offense that wasn't capable of playing catch-up football.

Our defense didn't let us down. We stopped the Rams' running game and put tremendous pressure on Gabriel, sometimes with a four-man rush, other times with an all-out blitz.

Offensively, we started slowly. Our first series ended with a punt from our own 39-yard line. Later, on second and eight from the Rams' 45-yard line, I sent Brown in and he hit John Mackey on a short pass for nine yards and a first down on the 36, but the drive ended with a missed field goal from 46 yards out.

Two more series failed, and we were forced to punt from our own territory, but each time our defense held. The scoring ice was broken early in the second quarter when Lou Michaels kicked a 50-yard field goal, and we led, 3-0.

Our defense forced a fumble, and we had the ball again on the Ram 36-yard line. A running play gained eight yards, and on second and two, Lenny Moore broke off tackle and went 28 yards to score against a Ram blitz. I looked up at the scoreboard, and we led, 10-0. Hard to believe, but there it was.

You could feel our players gaining confidence and sensing they could win.

There were still ten minutes remaining in the half, and we were able to contain the Rams until late in the period when they climaxed an 80-yard drive with a ten-yard touchdown pass from Gabriel to Tommy McDonald. Bruce Gossett added the extra point, and the half ended with the Colts leading 10-7.

I had nothing but praise for both our offensive and defensive units at halftime. Pleased with our three-point lead, I had no reason to change our game plan for the second half. We would continue to emphasize a ball control offense and an aggressive, swarming defense. Blitzing by the Rams was no longer a problem.

They used that tactic very little after Moore's touchdown run burned them.

We expected that the Rams, after being embarrassed in the first half, would be fired up and be much tougher during the final 30 minutes.

Early in the third period Gabriel went to work on us, passing 30 yards to Jack Snow, who made the catch on our 30-yard line, outmaneuvered one of our defensive backs on the ten and crossed the goal line to put the Rams ahead. Gossett's extra point made it 14-10.

We showed no signs of an offense during the entire third quarter, but our defense kept us in the ball game by bottling up the Rams.

The tide turned in our favor early in the fourth quarter when we came through with the big play of the game. On third down and six to go from our own 32, our spotters upstairs suggested we try to hit Mackey on a pass pattern splitting the Rams' zone defense. I sent Brown into the game with the call, and Ed tossed a perfect pass over the middle to Mackey, who out-raced two defenders and went all the way to put us out in front again. Michaels' extra point made it 17-14, Colts.

There was still plenty of time left, and now we had to keep the Rams out of field-goal range since a tie would be enough to knock us out of contention for the title.

Once again our defense was superb, stopping the Rams time and again. On offense, no one could have asked more of Matte. In fact, the rest of the fourth period was almost all Matte. You would have thought that he had been our quarterback all season. A quarterback statue was good for 20 yards, and a quarterback keeper picked up ten. A quarterback draw gained eight yards, and a quarterback bootleg fooled the Rams for 20 yards.

Not only did this ground game eat up valuable time, but it brought us close enough for Michaels to boot a 23-yard field goal to give us a 20-14 edge.

This took a little of the pressure off our defense since it meant the Rams could no longer go for the field goal.

It looked like the Rams might pull it out in the final minutes when they moved deep into our territory, but Bobby Boyd stopped the drive with an interception, and Matte ran out the clock.

We had won our impossible game. Winning is always great, but this victory had to be the greatest.

Some other glorious moments were ours that season. We faced Green Bay in the playoffs for the Western Division title and lost in a sudden-death overtime game on a disputed field goal, but we scored a devastating 35-3 victory over Dallas in the Playoff Bowl.

The Los Angeles game, however, remains foremost in my memory because each one of us stood up to be counted. We had every excuse to lose, but our team showed great character in overcoming adversity at its worst.

XIV

Bart Starr

Bart Starr, one of the greatest quarterbacks ever to perform in the National Football League, was handed his most difficult assignment in 1974 when he was chosen as the man to rebuild the Green Bay Packers.

The challenge to become head coach and general manager of the organization which he once help transform into a true dynasty as a player was one Bart Starr readily accepted.

Those who know Starr are confident that in due time he will restore Green Bay to its former prominent position in the NFL. Starr became accustomed to winning under the great Vince Lombardi, and he won't be satisfied until the Packers return to the top.

As quarterback of some of the greatest teams ever fielded in the NFL, Starr led the Packers to three consecutive NFL titles in 1965, 1966, and 1967, the first and only team to accomplish this feat. He also was the key to Green Bay's victories in the first two Super Bowls and was named the most valuable player in both games.

During his career, he set and still holds league records for lifetime passing efficiency, 57.42 percent; lowest percentage of passes intercepted in one season, 1.2 percent, set in 1966; and most consecutive passes attempted without interception, 294. He shares with Gary Wood the fewest passes intercepted in a season, three.

Starr has received the Jim Thorpe Award, the Byron White Award, and NFL Gladiator Award. He also was named Pro Football Player of the Decade by the Columbus Touchdown Club.

All these awards were bestowed upon a player who was a lowly 17th-round draft choice by the Packers out of the University of Alabama.

Starr was born in Montgomery, Ala., on January 9, 1934.

———————

Editor's Note: Before his untimely death in 1970, Vince Lombardi had selected Green Bay's 21-17 victory over Dallas in the 1967 NFL championship game as the greatest of all games he ever coached. This game also was picked by sportswriters and broadcasters as one of the greatest professional football games ever played. With Vince no longer with us to recall this game, we felt that the man best qualified to do this chapter was Bart Starr, the present Green Bay coach, who was quarterback and star of the win over Dallas. No Green Bay player was closer to Lombardi than Starr, and his description of that big Packer victory is undoubtedly similar to what Vince would have written.

Green Bay 21, Dallas 17

1967 NFL CHAMPIONSHIP GAME

By Bart Starr

There are a number of reasons why Coach Lombardi and just about everyone connected with the Packer organization would select our 21-17 win over Dallas as our greatest game.

It was an exceptionally well-played game despite the fact that it was played on one of the most bitterly cold days for any football game.

There was the excitement of Green Bay first leading by 14-0 and then trailing by 17-14, and there was the dramatic finish when we went for the touchdown instead of the easy field goal which would have tied the game to put us into overtime.

Winning also meant becoming the first team in modern times to gain three consecutive championships. We had failed to achieve this goal in 1963 after having won titles in 1961 and 1962, and now we had a second chance.

There also had been some speculation that this might be Coach Lombardi's final season, and it was important to all of us that his last game be a fitting climax to his accomplishments at Green Bay.

And finally, this was a year in which we had to fight back from adversity. The Packers had suffered a great deal because we had many injuries during the entire season. It seemed as though everything had been going against us to prevent us from winning the three consecutive championships. Time and again, we would fall behind in a game and have to play catch-up football to win. That's bound to take its toll on a team.

I can't remember an entire week during which every day of practice was so unbelievably cold. It was difficult for us, but the uncomfortable conditions were secondary to the importance of the game, and no one complained when Coach Lombardi stuck to his regular schedule of work-outs.

To substantially shorten any of the practices or change our schedule in any way was something none of us expected from our coach. Players become accustomed to certain routines in preparing for a game, and successful coaches stick to these regular procedures.

We knew that we had our work cut out for us against the Cowboys. The year before in Dallas, we barely beat them, 34-27, in a high-scoring game that saw them erase a big deficit and come close to beating us. They were an up-and-coming team, and they qualified to meet us again for the title by overwhelming Cleveland, 52-14, in the playoffs.

We had great respect for this Dallas team. Although some might have been deceived by Don Meredith's jovial attitude, we regarded him as a fine quarterback who played well in the big games. He had excellent receivers, and their passing game was made all the more effective because of their fine running game.

Our offensive game plan against Dallas was very similar to the one we had used the previous year. Coach Lombardi was a fundamentalist—he believed in doing a few things well, and never liked to depart from them.

However, when we faced Dallas with their "flex" defense, certain adjustments were necessary.

Their defensive alignment, for example, limited the effectiveness of our famous sweep play.

The uncomfortable week of practicing in the bitter cold failed to keep the emotion of our team from building to a peak. Coach Lombardi reminded us time and again that this was what we had been working for, and it was now down to one final game to determine if we could be the first team in modern times to win three championships in a row. We had been unable to accomplish this in 1963 and now we had been given a second chance. There are not too many times you get a second chance like this, and we were determined to make good.

In Green Bay, contrary to the pattern most teams follow the night before a game, we do not gather as a squad nor do we have a team breakfast the morning of the game. Following our Saturday practice, we return to our own homes and don't meet until a few hours before game time.

Before the game, Coach Lombardi met with the quarterbacks and as always reviewed what we would want to do in certain situations. These were never lengthy sessions. He always did such an outstanding job of preparing us all week that we were ready long before we took the field. There were never any last-minute changes. We would simply discuss things in general and make certain that if offered certain opportunities, we would be aware and take advantage of them.

Coach Lombardi was exceptional in his pre-game motivational speeches. When he addressed the team before a game, we listened and respected his words. His presence and timing always seemed to help us. Through the years, I don't think that anything he ever said hurt us in any way.

The week before, when we had played Los Angeles, he used a quote from the ninth chapter of the first Corinthians and repeated it to us all week. Its general theme was that many people run in a race but only one is going to win it, so run the race to the fullest so that you may win.

These same words from some other coach might not have had any impact on our players, but when we heard them from Coach Lombardi, they had a special meaning.

Even the way he re-emphasized that everything we had done for the past three years was now on the line, that playing under such severe weather conditions would be a true test of a championship team, were not regarded as cliches.

When Coach Lombardi spoke, it came from the heart, and we all knew it. He was no ordinary man.

The temperature was 13 degrees below zero at game time, and the wind was blowing at 15 miles per hour from out of the north. It was just awful. I've never been colder.

You never would have known that we were playing under such undesirable conditions as we put together an 82-yard drive for a touchdown the first time we got the ball.

We ran mostly up the middle or off tackle and mixed the running plays with some passes. Two receptions by Carroll Dale, one up the middle for 17 yards and the other down the left sidelines for 15, gave us a first down on the Dallas nine. After Donnie Anderson picked up a yard, I hit Boyd Dowler in the end zone for our first touchdown.

Early in the second period, we made it 14-0, going 65 yards in four plays. We had a third and one on the Dallas 45, and since we had been moving the ball well on the ground, the Cowboys expected another running play on a short yardage situation.

Dallas coach Tom Landry was a master at setting up a defense to stop short yardage plays so we decided to go for the big one. Fullback Ben Wilson faked a plunge into the line, and Dallas reacted as we had expected, moving in and trying to jam up the middle. Dowler raced down the field, managed to get behind Mel Renfro, the Dallas safety, and I threw the ball as hard as I could against the wind. Boyd picked it up on his fingertips and went in for the score.

We had scored on two of the first three possessions, but we knew better than to get overconfident because of this early comfortable lead. In a game like this when you get a two touchdown lead, I guess subconsciously you think about playing a conservative game, but you learn from experience that you must not lose your momentum.

On the next series when we got the ball again, we tried two passes without any success, and the next time, we passed twice, once for only four yards and once incomplete.

It was obvious that we weren't trying to sit on our lead, but Dallas had tightened up its coverage, and we weren't able to move the ball.

Dallas wasn't having any better luck either, and we kept

exchanging possession until I committed a costly fumble which gave them an easy touchdown.

From our own 26, I dropped back to pass and had good protection, but every receiver downfield was covered. I was thinking about throwing the ball away when I was hit by Willie Townes and fumbled the ball. George Andrie picked up the ball on the seven-yard line and ran in for the touchdown, and our lead was cut to 14-7.

Throw the football away, Coach Lombardi told me when I came off the field. Don't let that happen again, he warned.

Moments later, Willie Wood fumbled a punt on our 17, and Phil Clark recovered for Dallas. Less than a minute remained, but Danny Villanueva kicked a 21-yard field goal, and we took a mere four-point lead into the dressing room at half time.

None of us had been thinking about an easy romp when we were ahead, 14-0. All too clear in our minds was our game against Dallas the previous year when we had jumped off to a 14-0 lead only to find ourselves in a desperate battle down to the wire.

Two costly mistakes on this bitter cold day had put Dallas back in the ball game, but we were not disheartened. We were pros. We had been in championship games before and had played under tremendous pressure.

In the dressing room at half time, Coach Lombardi warned me again not to give them any turn-overs in our territory. We did not want to give them any more easy scores or put them in good field position.

I had been sacked four times during the first half because the Dallas coverage had improved and also because the field was getting harder, making it difficult for our receivers to break loose. In any event, Coach Lombardi made it clear that I should throw the ball away and not take such big losses.

Statistically, we were doing fine in the first half, and although it is encouraging, that doesn't always win ball games for you. Dallas had managed only three first downs to our nine and had gained only 42 yards to our 108, yet we were ahead by only four points.

Dallas came out for the second half a determined and

inspired team and dominated the play in the third quarter. They had two opportunities but failed to score while we floundered about and could pick up only one first down the entire period.

The momentum which had been all in our favor early in the game had switched, and on the first play of the final quarter, a 50-yard pass put Dallas in front, 17-14.

What hurt us the most was that they fooled us on an option pass play that we knew they had used successfully before. Halfback Dan Reeves took a pitch out from Meredith and swung to his left as though he was going to sweep around the end.

Bob Jeter, our cornerback, came up fast to stop the running play, but as he did, Reeves suddenly stopped and threw a long, high pass to Lance Rentzel, who was so far in the clear that he had to stop and wait for the ball. When Rentzel grabbed the ball, there was no way anyone was going to catch him.

Coach Lombardi was understandably upset about this big play. It was a situation that should not have happened . . . and did not usually happen to a Lombardi-coached team. Jeter's fast move towards Reeves was well-intentioned since he was hoping to nail the ball carrier for a big loss, but someone in the secondary failed to cover the territory that had been left open, and we were victimized.

There was still plenty of time to play, but the clock kept running down without our being able to regain our momentum. Thanks to a 15-yard penalty we were able to get within field-goal range midway in the period, but Chandler missed from 40 yards out, and we still trailed by three.

We got the ball on our 32 with 4:50 left in the game, and although we had not scored since early in the second period, Coach Lombardi felt confident that we would be able to pull it out. But more importantly, the players felt we could.

When we went into our huddle, I didn't say anything like "This may be our last chance, gang, so we've really got to go now." I looked around the huddle, and there was no need to say anything. Their eyes told me that they were determined to make this opportunity pay off.

A pass to Donnie Anderson gained six, and Chuck Mercein,

carrying the ball for the first time in the game, picked up seven and a first down on our 45.

A 13-yard pass to Dowler down the middle put the ball in Dallas territory on their 42. There was 3:30 left to play, and we were far from desperate. We were content to take whatever the Dallas defense would give us, and grind out the yardage in small chunks.

Our drive was stalled momentarily when Anderson was nailed for a nine-yard loss, putting us in a second and 19 situation from our 49. The Cowboys' linebackers were dropping very deep to cut off our crossing routes, and when I couldn't find the primary receiver open, I dumped the ball off to Anderson, who did some fancy running on the icy turf to pick up 12 yards.

It was now third and seven on the Dallas 39 with two minutes to go. I faded back to pass, and once again the primary receiver was covered so I went to Anderson again, and he picked up the necessary yardage for the first down plus two additional yards to keep our drive alive.

We had a first down on the 30 with 1:33 left. Chuck Mercein, a sharp, astute player, came back to huddle to say the linebackers were so deep, he could catch the ball underneath them for a big gain, so stay alert for him. I was able to spot Mercein open just over the line and lofted a short pass to him. Chuck Howley came up fast and almost nailed Mercein, but Mercein made a great move and raced down the field, going out-of-bounds on the 11 to stop the clock.

Now, there was 1:11 left to play, and being in certain field-goal range, there would be no more passing. We had trouble running against defensive tackle Bob Lilly as everyone did, so we decided to try to fool him. Gale Gillingham, our guard, pulled out to the right, and Lilly, sensing a run to the right, went with him. I handed the ball off to Mercein, who bolted through the hole left vacant by Gillingham and Lilly, and Chuck made it down to the three for an eight-yard gain. A great block by Bob Skoronski on George Andre insured the success of the play. This play gave me more satisfaction than any I ever called.

There were 54 seconds left on the clock. Anderson got us the first down on the one on a drive play. There were 30 seconds left. We called the same play, and this time Donnie was held without any gain. There were 20 seconds left. We tried Donnie once more on the same drive play, but the footing was treacherous, and he failed to gain again.

It was third and goal to go from the one, but only 16 seconds remained. We called our final time out and went to the sidelines to talk with Coach Lombardi.

Earlier in the game, we had run what we called the 31 wedge play with the fullback going over tackle on short yardage plays. We had been able to pick up a minimum of two yards on this play by handling one of their tackles who for some reason always played far too high on short yardage situations instead of getting underneath the blockers.

This was our lead play on short yardage for this game, but because that end of the field is not exposed to much sunlight late in the year, it had become very hard and very slippery, and the proper footing for the needed fast start by either running back was hopeless.

I mentioned all this to Coach Lombardi and said that if our guard, Jerry Kramer, could get his footing so that he could make the necessary block, I would be able to sneak it over since I could get to the hole much quicker than the fullback who was three yards behind me.

Coach Lombardi said fine, and that was it. We never even discussed the possibility of a field goal which would have tied the game and sent it into overtime. I was so sure that the play was going to work that we never stopped to think that with no times out left and the clock running, there might not be time enough to get the field goal team in there if we failed.

When I went back to the huddle, I asked Jerry if he was absolutely sure he could get his footing to make the block, and when he said he could, I called the quarterback sneak on an improvised 31 wedge play.

Jerry made what probably was the biggest block of his great career, and I fortunately was able to get enough traction so that I could make it over the goal line.

In the dressing room after the game, it was a strange, almost subdued atmosphere. There was no bedlam, no whooping or hollering. We were, of course, all happy, but we were all drained emotionally. It was difficult to have the kind of first time enthusiasm you display after winning a big championship. I don't mean to imply that we were blase or took it all for granted.

It was the sort of feeling that "Well, we did it, gang. . . three in a row, but man, am I ever drained." It had been a tough year for us, and it had been an especially tough game for us against Dallas.

But most important, it was a fitting climax to Lombardi's career as a coach at Green Bay for it was the last game he coached in our stadium.

Lombardi had come to Green Bay as head coach in 1959, took a team that had finished 1-10-1 the previous year and through his leadership and direction, help us finish 7-5 his first season. In 1960, we were Conference champions, and the following year, we were the world's champions.

He was a strict disciplinarian and had a very fundamental approach to the game. He was determined to keep our system simple, not only for the players to execute but for them to understand as well. That way, he believed, we would always keep our mistakes to an absolute minimum.

He stressed the need to block and tackle better than our opponents. He drove us to such a degree during our practices that many of the players felt the actual game was a reprieve.

He was never as tough on us following a defeat as he was when we won, prompting some to look around in amazement as if to ask themselves if we had actually won.

Though he was tough, demanding, unrelenting and even abrasive, he was compassionate, sensitive, and extremely fair. Everyone respected his knowledge of the game and the outstanding leadership qualities that he possessed, and all who played for him are better men today.

He was the greatest, and will long be remembered not only for his greatest victory on December 31, 1967, but for being a rare human being.

XV

Hank Stram

After serving 15 years as head coach of the Kansas City Chiefs (originally the Dallas Texans), Henry "Hank" Stram embarked on a new career in 1975 as analyst for the telecast of NFL games on CBS.

But you couldn't keep Stram away from the coaching sidelines very long. In 1976, he was named vice-president and head coach of the New Orleans Saints and given the challenging task of building a winner for a franchise which had never come close to a winning season since it was organized in 1967.

Stram's success with the Chiefs earned him Coach of the Year honors in 1962, 1966, 1968, and 1969. His teams won three American Football League titles, Super Bowl IV, and had the distinction of being the first AFL team to play in the Super Bowl.

With a record of 124 victories, he is the third most winning active coach in the NFL today.

After his 1948 graduation from Purdue where he won the Big Ten medal for best individual combining athletics with scholarship, Stram stayed witht he Boilermakers for eight years as backfield coach. He moved to Southern Methodist in 1956 for one season, then spent two years at Notre Dame and one at Miami (Fla.) as an assistant coach.

In 1960, he was named head coach of the new Dallas Texans in the American Football League. The Texans moved to Kansas City in 1963.

Stram is regarded as one of the leading innovators in professional football.

He was born in Chicago on January 3, 1924, but spent most of his youth in Gary, Ind.

Kansas City 23, Minnesota 7

1970 SUPER BOWL IV

By Hank Stram

If I had been asked before January 11, 1970, to select my most memorable game as a pro coach, I would have chosen the 1962 American Football League Championship which was the first league title of my career. As the Dallas Texans, we defeated the defending champion Houston Oilers, 20-17, after 15 minutes and 54 seconds of sudden-death overtime. For sheer excitement, tension, and drama, that game is difficult to match. We had a 17-0 half-time lead, but they tied the score in the second half. Tommy Brooker's 25-yard field goal finally gave us the victory in the longest professional football game ever played.

I also would have given consideration to our 1967 appearance in the first Super Bowl game, even though we lost to Green Bay 35-10.

That game rates among my most memorable ones for a number of reasons. First, I felt it was a great honor to be the first American Football League representative in the Super Bowl. I had been in the league since its inception in 1960, and we had been looking forward to opposing the NFL champions for some time. There was further significance in the fact that LaMar Hunt, our club owner, was the founder of the AFL, and it was a great challenge for all of us to be playing against Green Bay, then the glamour team of professional football and one of the best pro teams in a long, long time.

Even though I will always reserve a special place in my

memories for these two games, they have to make room for the 1970 Super Bowl in New Orleans where we defeated the Minnesota Vikings, 23-7, for the world championship of professional football.

The year before, the New York Jets had become the first American Football League team to win the Super Bowl by beating Baltimore 16-7, but there were still quite a few football fans who were skeptical about that win by the Jets.

Certainly the oddsmakers were foremost among the disbelievers.

As a coach, you don't pay much attention to the odds listed in the newspapers, although you can't help but be aware of them. I thought it was peculiar that even before the oddsmakers had known the opposing teams in the 1970 Super Bowl, the NFL was made a 13- or 14-point favorite, which meant to me that they were still basing their judgments on leagues instead of people.

That's a mistake some people have been making since the inception of our league. I feel very strongly about the fact that pro football is not a game of insignias, nor is it a game of leagues. It is a game of people, and as a result it was hard for me to understand how anyone could justifiably say that one team was going to be a 13-point underdog because of its league.

However, I think we made believers out of most of them. We entered the game as a very confident football team. We had grown considerably since the first Super Bowl game, and developed greatly as far as maturity, poise, and confidence are concerned.

I think that we all relate to experiences, and the fact that we could relate to a Super Bowl experience, even though we hadn't succeeded, helped us immeasurably.

During the week prior to the Super Bowl, I was very upset with the way our quarterback, Len Dawson, had been linked unfairly to a gambling investigation. It was a very irresponsible charge, and created some anxious and trying hours. It put great pressure on Lennie, much more so on him than it did our squad and staff. This kind of thing could work against or be an advantage to a team. It would certainly be a big burden on a young team, but ours was not a young team emotionally, and Lennie responds to pressure and adversity as well as any player I have ever coached. Because of my great confidence in Lennie and our entire squad and because of the many adversities we had overcome during the season, I didn't think this would really be a problem.

I told our squad before we started the season that any time a group of 40 people work for six months to achieve a goal, there is bound to be adversity, but we had to be strong enough to overcome these adversities and continue to win.

For example: we lost Dawson for six games and then we lost our back-up quarterback, Jackie Lee, because of injuries. I told the squad that we couldn't insulate ourselves with a reason to fail just because of an injury. We would still have to find a way to win. As a result, the team rallied around each other, maintained a great feeling of confidence and poise and continued to play with a strong purpose—to win. The maturity with which we reacted during the season carried over to this game.

When the story on Dawson broke, we had that same feeling of confidence. Even though there was concern among all of us, I thought it was important for us to clear the air so that we could concentrate all of our attention and efforts on the game. We did just that by calling a press conference.

The press conference cleared the air, and we worked and prepared without any ill effects.

Part of our pre-game practice was, of course, devoted to working out a plan to stop Joe Kapp. We thought it was important to keep Kapp in the pocket as much as we could. Looking at the films it became very evident to us that he could move by design and throw on the run as well as anyone we had seen all year.

We decided to use our triple stack defense, which is an over-shifted defense to the strong side. Structurally speaking, the defense is one whereby we move our defensive ends, Jerry Mays and Aaron Brown, from the inside position of the tight end to a position outside the tight end. We call this our odd spacing which means that we would have Buck Buchanan or Curley Culp on the nose of their center, Mick Tinglehoff. We hoped that these two aspects of our defensive approach to the game would prevent Kapp from doing an effective job on his rollouts, and they did. Although Kapp completed 16 of 25 passes, most were fairly short. He ran only twice for a total of nine yards, and he was dropped three times for a total of 21 yards in losses.

We felt that Minnesota's tight end would hurt us more than their outside receivers, since we are basically a zone defense team and use that type of coverage most of the time. We were right about that as their great receiver, Gene Washington, caught only one pass and that one for only nine yards. He was so well covered that they threw to him only three times all afternoon.

Our offensive game plan was a fairly simple one. We thought that it was very important to double team both defensive ends on all of our short passing attempts. This was something we had never done before, but we knew their cornerbacks played a little soft, and we wanted to throw in front of them and throw quickly so that they would not disturb the flight of the ball.

We were aware that their defensive ends had great range and were good leapers. We knew that if we did not double team them, there was a danger of the ends knocking the ball down.

We also double teamed them on all of the off-tackle plays and on plays we ran right at them. We wanted to run directly at them because they read plays, reacted, and pursued as well as anybody we had seen.

We also wanted to use some misdirection plays. We used a variety of end-around plays from different formations during the regular season, but the ones we used so successfully against Minnesota were plays we hadn't used too much before. Oddly enough, these end-arounds which turned out so well for us in the Super Bowl weren't too successful during the season.

We decided to go on a quick count because it would change the tempo of the Minnesota defense. We ran on quick counts 27 times during the game, and this was very effective.

We used 17 different offensive formations, but basically we

did not deviate too much from the approach we had used all year. For example, we used 21 formations against Oakland.

I was hoping that we would win the toss and get a chance to get on the scoreboard first, but we lost and kicked off to Minnesota. Kapp moved his team well, and the Vikings went from their own 20 to our 39 where we held. On fourth down, with the wind against them, Minnesota decided to punt instead of trying for the field goal, and we went on the offensive for the first time.

We were able to advance to Minnesota's 41 where the Vikings' defense stiffened. Jan Stenerud kicked a Super Bowl record 48-yard field goal, which gave us a 3-0 lead with a little over eight minutes gone in the first quarter.

Late in the first quarter, we started a drive from our own 20 and moved 55 yards to Minnesota's 25 where we were stopped. Stenerud was called on again and came through with a 32-yard field goal to give us a 6-0 lead with 13:20 left in the half.

It wasn't too much later that we got another drive going and, helped by a 19-yard run by Frank Pitts on a flanker reverse, we were able to get down to the Minnesota 18.

Once again, we were unable to go all the way, and this time Stenerud kicked a 25-yard field goal to increase our lead to 9-0 with 7:52 left in the half.

On the ensuing kickoff, Charley West fumbled the ball, and Remi Prudhomme recovered for us on the Minnesota 19.

Dawson went right to work, trying to get us our first touchdown, but he was thrown for an eight-yard loss attempting to pass. On a quick count, quick opening play from the I formation, Wendell Hayes picked up 13 yards. Dawson rolled out to the right and passed to flanker Otis Taylor down the right sideline for ten yards and a first down on the four.

Mike Garrett lost a yard and then was stopped at the line of scrimmage. On third down, Garrett went over from the five on what we called our 65 toss power trap.

On this play, our left tackle, Jim Tyrer, pulled to influence his man, Alan Page. Page came through, and our right guard, Mo

Moorman, pulled and took him out of the play with an inside-out trap block. Our tight end, Fred Arbanas, took care of their middle linebacker, enabling Garrett to score off-tackle after taking a short pitch from Dawson.

Stenerud's extra point made it 16-0 at 9:26 of the period, and that's the way the score remained the rest of the half.

During halftime, I told our squad that we had been working toward this goal since we first started our preseason weight lifting program back in March. Now it boiled down to just 30 minutes, and the remaining 30 minutes of the game would probably be the most important minutes of our lives—and nobody was going to take it away from us.

Even though we had a 16-0 lead and had moved the ball well in the first half, we were concerned about the second half since we had seen how Minnesota had been able to come back against the Los Angeles Rams.

We left the dressing room at halftime with the idea of not being conservative. We felt we could not sit on our 16-0 lead. We wanted to stay on the offensive. We were going to throw the ball and continue to do the things that we thought we could do going into the game.

We received the second half kickoff and had possession of the ball for the first six minutes but couldn't get another score.

When Minnesota took over on their own 31, they moved 60 yards in ten plays, with Dave Osborn going over from the four. Fred Cox added the extra point to cut our lead down to 16-7 at 10:28 of the third period.

Kapp had looked especially good during the drive as he passed to John Beasley for 15, Bill Brown for 11, and finally to Oscar Reed for 12 and a first down on our four.

We knew that Minnesota was hot and that we had to put out the fire, so we went right to work recapturing complete control of the game.

Starting from our 18 after the ensuing kickoff, we moved to the 32 on four plays and were faced with a big third down and seven yards to go. Frank Pitts took the ball on a flanker reverse and barely picked up the first down as he was run out of bounds on our 39. A 15-yard penalty for roughing the passer moved the ball to Minnesota's 46 where Dawson passed to Otis Taylor in the flat, and Otis went all the way for the touchdown.

The pass itself covered only five yards out to the right, and Taylor was almost nailed at the 41. But he broke away from cornerback Earsell Mackbee, and then raced past Karl Kassulke, Minnesota's safety. It was truly a great individual effort typical of Otis.

Stenerud's extra point made it 23-7 and the scoring for the day was over at 13:38 of the third quarter.

Our defense could not have been better the remainder of the game as we picked off three interceptions and did not allow Minnesota to get closer than our 46-yard line.

It was a great victory, and made me extremely proud of our team. Football is a game of attitude. Ability alone will not win championships. Our players not only reached down and gave us 100 percent of their true ability, but they also had the proper attitude. Each player made every personal sacrifice necessary for the success of the team. They were totally committed and completely involved in being champions.

We became the world champions of professional football on January 11, 1970, because we had 40 dedicated people playing with great spirit, discipline, unity, and determination; and because of the great effort and maturity shown by our squad, the Super Bowl victory will long live as my most memorable game as a pro coach.